BASIC CONCEPTS IN SOCIOLOGY

MAX WEBER

BASIC CONCEPTS IN SOCIOLOGY

Translated and with an Introduction by
H. P. SECHER

**THE
CITADEL
PRESS**

NEW YORK

FIFTH PAPERBOUND EDITION JANUARY, 1968

The Citadel Press
222 Park Avenue South
New York 3, N. Y.

LIBRARY OF CONGRESS CATALOGUE CARD NO.: 61-15252

CONTENTS

Max Weber was born on April 21, 1864, in Erfurt, Thuringia (now East Germany), the eldest son of a well situated German family that valued education, culture and citizenship. Max was surrounded by good books from the day he was born and by the time he was fourteen could and did read Homer, Virgil, and Livy fluently in the original. By the time he finished the Gymnasium he had read his way through the forty-volume Weimar edition of Goethe's works, could quote Shakespeare in English and had exercised his critical faculties on the works of Spinoza, Schopenhauer and Kant. Weber began his serious studies at the University of Heidelberg on the faculty of law, but his interests carried over into the fields of economics and philosophy, in all of which he regularly attended lectures.

Despite such a prodigious interest in learning, Weber's student days do not present a uniform picture of the budding bookworm. Max could not make up his mind whether to lead the life of the scholar or that of the gentleman. Probably in order to overcome his ascetic tendencies he joined one of the *Burschenschaften* (duelling fraternities) and quickly adopted their boisterous way of life and shallow nationalistic views. The picture of crude animal spirit that he presented on one of his visits home was enough to anger his mother into trying to slap some sense of decency back into him. The effect was lasting. This phase and the incident are important because they signify Weber's continuous dilemma of having to choose between the life of scholarly isolation and that of personal involvement. Whenever he ventured too far afield from his chosen scholarly labors to become involved into political activities, a form of allegorical slap in the face always seemed to await him in the end!

In 1883, Weber began his year of voluntary military training that opened up reserve officer's status to university trained persons. Though he detested military service, he did not rebel— the part of him which enjoyed the fraternities acquiesced to the rigors and idiocies of military drill. When he finished his military training, he did not return to Heidelberg but matriculated at Berlin. In Berlin he came under the influence of Gneist and Gierke, absorbing from the former a feeling for British parliamentary institutions and from the latter an understanding of German legal history and the role played in it by associations; but he also listened with mixed feelings to Treitschke's crude nationalism. After a brief stay at Goettingen, Weber returned to Berlin in 1866, where he took his examination in law and reluctantly accepted a position at a Berlin criminal court. Since the work bored him, he continued his studies with Professor Mommsen and eventually wrote his Ph.D. dissertation. This dissertation was entitled *A Contribution to the History of Medieval Business Organizations*, and it already showed his skillful handling of legal concepts, economic principles and historical documentation. At his oral examination Professor Mommsen paid him high compliments and foresaw a brilliant career as a scholar for Weber.

But Weber was still uncertain whether an academic career could command his full attention. J. P. Mayer, in his study *Max Weber and German Politics* (London, 1944), wrote in this respect: "The conflict whether he should turn to practical things or whether he should pursue the aim of achieving something outstanding in the field of scholarship and academic teaching—and only an outstanding achievement would satisfy him—is profound. This conflict is, as it were, of constitutional significance for Max Weber's whole being." Weber was far from espousing a life of monastic asceticism; to him theoretical work acquired meaning only in the course of application and from this probably derived his later concern with scientific methodology rather than with metaphysical speculations.

Still torn between his desires to become involved in more worldly affairs or to pursue a purely academic career, Weber prepared his habilitation study in order to qualify as an instructor in Law at the University of Berlin. This effort, constituting his second major work, took the form of a study of Roman agrarian history, but was really a penetrating analysis of the social, political and economic developments of Roman society. It was published in 1891.

While he was still working on the study and during his preparations for his tasks as instructor at the University of Berlin, Weber joined the *Verein für Sozialpolitik*. This association aimed at the improvement of labor's working conditions, regulation of banking and business practices and was generally prepared to grant the state greater latitude in its handling of social problems. The members of this association became known as *Katheder Sozialisten* (academic socialists), an early German version of the British Fabian society. In the *Verein* Weber found at least a limited outlet for his desire to combine theoretical investigations with practical applications and through these activities he became thoroughly conversant with the sociopolitical problems of his day.

9

In 1892, Weber married Marianne Schnitger and formally began his lectures at the University of Berlin. Two years later, Weber was offered and accepted a full professorship at the University of Freiburg. There he delivered his inaugural lecture in 1895 on *The National State and Germanic Policy*, which, in its essentials, forecast much of his later political thinking. His central point, as relevant then as it is now, was the question of whether the German bourgeoisie was politically mature enough to take on the political leadership of the nation. Though Weber answered it in the negative, he doubted that it was really too late to make good this lack of political education. But he admonished his listeners that the task was immense and that it must remain the serious duty of every German, "each in his narrow circle," to collaborate in the political education of his nation. Political education, he declared, must be the goal of political science.

Very soon afterwards Weber was appointed Professor of Economics at Heidelberg University, where he spent one of his intellectually most fruitful and enjoyable years. But within the year Weber suffered a nervous breakdown which resulted in the complete suspension of his work. For hours, his wife and biographer recalled later in her *Max Weber, Ein Lebensbild* (Tübingen, 1926), he would sit at the window and stare into space; his recovery took almost four years, during which time he never opened a book or wrote a line. Weber again returned to his scholarly labors in 1903, at which time he began a long series of studies to clarify the method of the social sciences. He was also appointed associate editor of the *Archiv für Sozialwissenschaften*, which flowered into Germany's foremost journal of the social sciences, a position which it held until the advent of Hitler.

In 1904, Weber made his first visit to the United States, to attend a scientific World Congress held in St. Louis. In the United States Weber thought he recognized the meaning of the Twentieth Century: the ascendency of the masses and the need of vast bureaucratic structures to govern them. The same year also saw the publication of his *The Protestant Ethic and the Spirit of Capitalism*. In this work Weber analyzed the beginnings of capitalism in order to gain a fuller appreciation of the significance and implications of capitalist economics in its contemporary phase. Weber foresaw the absence of any justification—religious or ethical—in the pursuit of wealth and feared its transformation in the United States into a mere sport, ending, possibly, in what he called "mechanized petrifaction."

Though the University of Heidelberg continued his appointment after his recovery, Weber was no longer able to lecture and in 1907, thanks to a substantial inheritance, he resigned and continued his work as a private scholar. The remaining years of his life were taken up with his studies of *Economics and Society*, in which he introduced the theme of the evolution of Western civilization in terms of its developing rationality and attempted to illuminate the emergence of industrial civilization, with emphasis on the characteristics that distinguish it from other, earlier forms of society. For the first time, according to Weber, the world witnessed the creation of a deliberately planned social order through the instrumentalities of capitalism in the economic sphere, the methods of science in the intellectual and the manipulation of bureaucracy in the political sphere.

Weber interrupted this work once during World War I, when he served in the administration of army hospitals, an experience

11

which provided him with rich materials for the formulation of principles on bureaucratic systems, and again in 1918, when he accepted an appointment as consultant to the German Armistice Commission, and as expert advisor on the Confidential Committee for Constitutional Reform. The result of this latter experience, Weber's last brush with the world of politics, was the eventual introduction into the Weimar constitution of Article 41, which provided for the election of the President by popular vote. It represented the culmination of much of Weber's thinking on this subject; he regarded the position of President of the new Reich as the focal point for the development of charismatic leadership which, he felt, could emerge only if that office was open to election by all the people. A popular leader must be the center of any political system and not an institution whose authority was only delegated, i.e., a parliamentary assembly. As the ignominious use of Article 48 (emergency powers) by the popularly elected President later showed, Weber had completely and romantically misread the true meaning of "plebiscitarian democracy." Nevertheless his death in June, 1920, at the age of 56 came at a time when his involvement in the political education of his countrymen might have been of considerable benefit to them. More than any other figure later during the Weimar period, Weber had the intellectual stature and respect that might have commanded him a hearing when the first danger signs of catastrophe began to appear.

At his death Max Weber left behind him a number of incomplete studies, including his *Wirtschaft und Gesselschaft (Economics and Society)*. Though most of these studies were far-ranging in scope and detailed in execution, there was among them one which represented, in effect, an effort by Weber to provide a set of definitions that would help to integrate his work and would also serve as a suitable introduction to it for the beginner. Since many of these definitions and principles were based on Weber's own empirical investigations, they had in fact been tested, and could be viewed as preliminary formulations for a general science of social behavior. Such a formulation had been, for example, his statement on sociology which appeared in the journal *Logos*, Vol. IV (1913), and it is the reworked version of this article that makes up the following pages. This latter version was written shortly before his death and published posthumously as Chapter I of *Wirtschaft und Gesellschaft* (in "Grundriss der Sozialekonomik," Part III, Tübingen, 1925).

These methodological principles begin with Weber's definition of sociology as the science which aims at the interpretative understanding of social behavior in order to gain an explanation of its causes, its course and its effects. The rest of the study is mainly concerned with the explanation of what is meant by such terms as social behavior, understanding, causal explanation, and what typological means must be used for purposes of analysis. Here we can only briefly sketch the salient points of Weber's systematization. Readers who are interested in a fuller treatment are referred to the excellent studies by Theodore Able, *Systematic Sociology in Germany* (New York, 1929); Reinhard Bendix, *Max Weber, An Intellectual Portrait* (Garden City, 1960); H. Gerth and C. W. Mills, eds., *From Max Weber: Essays in Sociology* (New York, 1946); and A. M. Henderson and T. Parsons, eds., *Max Weber: The Theory of Social and Economic Organization* (Glencoe, 1947).

According to Weber, human conduct, in order to qualify as social behavior must be clearly *intentional*, i.e., it must have meaning attached to it by the individuals engaged in it, who in turn orient themselves toward the similar behavior of others. Merely introspective conduct such as meditation, or conduct that is oriented toward material objects or situations ranks only as nonsocial behavior (Par. 1, B). In order to analyze social behavior Weber proceeds to create certain typical ideal behavior patterns for purposes of comparison with actual examples of behavior that he had observed in his investigations.

We are thus introduced to Weber's term of the *ideal type*, by which he proposes that all conceptual formulations and definitions in sociology should be expressed (Par. 1, A, sec. 11). Such an ideal type is created by means of "a one-sided emphasis and intensification of one or several aspects of a given event and represents a uniform mental structure" (Able). Weber is quite insistent on making clear that such an ideal type must be at least in the realm of probability and not merely possible; that is, there must be found somewhere at least a close empirical approximation. Thus, the construction of an ideal type can also be regarded as a working hypothesis, which, until its realistic worth has been proved by observation, may, like any other hypothesis, be of little analytical value. The ideal type, furthermore, is purely *descriptive* and should not be misused to explain the data it reveals; nor does it at any time indicate what action can or should be taken.

The ideal type is therefore primarily an instrument for classification, and as such useful for the systematic arrangement of several categories in each of which all observations—either quantitatively or qualitatively—that are covered by its descriptions may be grouped together. In this way it is possible, for example, to construct ideal types of bureaucracy, feudalism, parliamentary democracy or capitalism and then classify the observational data according to their greater proximity to one of these types rather than to others.

The most important form of social behavior according to Weber is so-called reciprocal social behavior, which terminologically becomes a *social relation* and whose study is considered by Weber to be the central theme of sociology. A social relation is present where individuals mutually base their behavior on the expected behavior of others (Par. 3). Some of the types of social relations that Weber singles out for explanation in the following pages are struggle, communalization, aggregation and corporate groups (Pars. 8, 9, 10).

Struggle he defines as a form of social relation in which one individual behaves in such a way as to assert his will over and against the resistance of another individual. *Communalization* is a social relation based upon a subjective feeling, either emotional or traditional, of belonging together. *Aggregation* is a social relationship based upon a rationally motivated balance or a union of interests. A *corporate group*, in turn, constitutes a social relation in which authority is upheld by the activities of a leader and an administrative staff. The last three types of social relationships may be either *open* or *closed*, depending on whether participation in them is due to voluntary agreement or to authoritative imposition.

Undoubtedly one of the more complex terms in Weber's vocabulary of definitions is that of "understanding." It is difficult to render this term in English since here it is used in a much broader sense than the one which Weber reserves for it. According to Weber a course of behavior may have an intended meaning, regardless of whether or not a person or persons involved in it "understands" the meaning of their behavior. Neither does the observer of a course of behavior always "understand" its meaning. The chief point of meaningful behavior is simply that some "intention" is attached to it (Par. 1, A, secs. 1, 2, 3). Obviously certain actions are carried out with a more clearly defined purpose than others, and the means employed to achieve their goals are clearly discernible. Thus a reflex action is "meaningless" as the direction of that action may not be the one originally intended and the means to bring it about have not been selected with forethought. As usual Weber warns that there is no rigid separation between "meaningful" behavior and behavior that has no intent attached to it.

The importance of "understanding" lies for Weber in its strictly technical nature of providing a clue to the observation and theoretical interpretation of the subjective states of mind of individuals whose behavior is being studied. In other words "understanding" becomes a tool of sociological research which aims at providing more insight than can be had, even by the most precise statistical proof, of the high correlation between a given situation and a corresponding course of behavior. "Understanding" goes further by asking not only why an action has taken place but also why a certain "behavior pattern" continues to be followed. In this way the search for motivation is introduced as basic to any kind of sociological interpretation. Merely functional understanding may suffice for the natural sciences, but not for the social sciences, which must probe the why and wherefore of any given course of social behavior (Par. 1, A, sec. 9).

Thus, the discovery that a capacity for rational conduct is correlated with a specific cephalic index and that where such correlation exists there can be noted a greater desire for power and prestige is merely a *datum* of and not an *object* for sociological investigation. Sociological analysis begins only with the causal explanation of the *kind* of social behavior that leads to the acquisition of power and prestige by showing such correlation, why or why not they succeeded in their undertaking, and what were the understandable consequences of their seeking of power under equally "meaningful" behavior of other individuals. It is necessary therefore to gain knowledge of the whole social situation and not merely of isolated conditions or events, however uniform their appearance may be.

Weber insists that even though the process of "understanding" is essentially subjective, the individual engaging in it can do so with the necessary degree of objective detachment. Of course, because the individual can never detach himself completely from other individuals whose social behavior he is interpreting, such interpretation will necessarily always be more fragmentary and hypothetical than a similar process of causal interpretation in the natural sciences. But in recognizing this difficulty, Weber also suggests means of overcoming it. He does this by distinguishing interpretation which is merely *adequate at the level of meaning* (i.e., it gives some single sufficient reason for a certain type of behavior), from interpretation which is also *causally adequate*. A causally adequate interpretation is achieved when the probability of a recurrence of a phenomenon under the same circumstance is empirically determined. Thus, in order for sociology to achieve scientifically balanced explanation it must use both criteria of adequacy on the level of meaning and causal adequacy because "If no meaning attaches itself to such typical behavior, then no matter how high the degree of uniformity or the statistical preciseness of probability, it still remains an incomprehensible statistical probability regardless of whether it deals with an overt or subjective process" (Par. 1, A, sec. 7).

Weber suggests two *ways* by which "understanding" is obtained and two *kinds* of "understanding" that have to be taken into consideration. Thus we may understand the meaning of a given type of behavior intellectually if the behavior is rational. Such rationality depends on the behavior pattern unfolding in a manner that to us appears to be logical, i.e., it conforms to a predictable sequence of behavior. Again we may acquire "understanding" by empathy of a given type of behavior if such behavior appears to be irrational. Such empathy is achieved by projecting oneself into the irrational situation and experiencing its emotional impact. The more susceptible we are ourselves to a given type of irrationality, the more readily will such "understanding" occur (Par. 1, A, sec. 3).

By using either the intellectual or empathic approach we can achieve two *kinds* of "understanding." By mere observation of a familiar action we can obtain *actual understanding* (e.g., a person who reaches for the knob to shut a door). This is probably the most common form of understanding. Or we can try to discover the motives underlying the conduct just observed and in this way achieve what Weber calls *explanatory understanding*. In order to establish a meaningful connection between the performance of an act and its underlying motive, the observer must be able to project himself intellectually and emotionally into the same situation, with the knowledge that under similar conditions he would behave in the same way. To *actually understand* the meaning of a familiar form of conduct is merely an exercise in deduction. But to explain the motives behind it will always be a difficult fundamental question of methodology in the social sciences—difficult because any concern with motives must remain necessarily always incomplete, since even the individual engaging in a certain form of behavior may not always be aware of his own motivation. Thus it would not be unusual for the same situation to be explainable in terms of two entirely different sets of motivation, each of which appears equally valid to the observer.

Weber's passion for scientific objectivity left him when he turned to a consideration of the state. Here his definition seems to echo the influence of Hegel, Treitschke and the high-pitched nationalism of the Wilhelmine empire.

Already in his inaugural lecture at the University of Freiburg, Weber had declared that "the power and interests of the nation are the last and decisive interests which economic policy has to serve. . . . The national state is for us the secular power organization of the nation and in this national state the *raison d'état* is for us the ultimate yardstick for economic considerations." Marianne Weber also informs us that "His passion for the national power state sprang clearly from an innate instinct which no reasoning could call into question. The powerful nation is the expanded body of a powerfully endowed man; its affirmation is his self-affirmation." The *Machtstaat* idea was, according to J. P. Mayer, central to Weber's admiration of Bismarck as the faithful and brilliant practitioner of Machiavellism. Hans Kohn, who in his *The Mind of Germany* (New York, 1960), subjects Weber's liberalism to searching criticism, noted that "Weber, like most German scholars, never understood the implications and limitations of Machiavellism. He was unable to see the moral element inherent in any political power."

Accordingly, Weber's definition of the state rests primarily on authority, bureaucracy, compulsory jurisdiction over a territory and monopolization of the legitimate use of force (Par. 17, sec. 3). He is careful to reject any definition of the modern state and its legal order that centers on either the purpose of the political community or some specific value judgments that inspire belief in its legitimacy. Instead he states that political communities have pursued all conceivable ends at one time or another without thereby losing the character of the modern state. All political formations are formations of violence to Weber, with the state singled out especially "as the last source of all legitimate violence."

"Power" Weber defines as the opportunity which permits one individual to impose his will on the behavior of others even against their will. But he rejects his definition as being too elusive, in favor of the narrower concept of "domination," which is in effect political power (Par. 16). Domination is achieved by influencing others through the explicit articulation of what one wants them to do and having these "commands" obeyed implicitly. However the two way relationship between ruler and ruled which this concept implies hinges on the belief by both sides in the legitimacy of the authority that exercises domination. Consequently, Weber considered it necessary to recognize three principles which permit this legitimate exercise of the power to issue commands.

He distinguished "charismatic" leadership, which depended on the personal magnetism of the leader and which arose in response to crises from the two other, more stable, types of authority. These he defined as "traditional" authority, based upon hereditary leadership and the appeal to tradition—for example in the case of patrimonialism and feudalism—and "legal" authority, in which domination was based on formal rules and objective standards of justice (Par. 7). These are, of course, typical examples of Weber's *ideal types* and he cautioned that charismatic leadership no sooner arises in any society than it tends to become routinized into the traditional or legal pattern, though in a new crisis another charismatic leader might take command once more. In Western society generally, Weber observed a moving away from traditional to legal authority with an increasing tendency in modern society to displace the rule of law by a more bureaucratized system of administration.

It would be pointless in this short treatment of Weberian concepts to follow them through their labyrinthine meanings and interpretations. *The Basic Concepts of Sociology* must necessarily stand as an unfinished and highly fragmentary attempt at systematization. As Bendix correctly points out, the set of definitions contained in this late generalizing effort of Weber's should not be considered in isolation from his other works, to which, indeed, it refers constantly, if not always clearly. It provides, however, a good, albeit incomplete, introduction to the thinking of Max Weber, with important clues to concepts that are much more fully developed in his other works. To the novice who has heard vaguely about Max Weber—and also about Alfred, his nearly equally illustrious brother, but finds it difficult to distinguish between the two—it should prove an excellent beginning and a stimulus to tackle not only Max Weber's original studies but also the work of some of his commentators.

It is primarily with this purpose in mind that this translation has been undertaken. Rendering Weber into readable English has often been characterized as a linguist's nightmare. Driven by a passion for preciseness, Weber involutes his sentences, introduces a myriad of qualifying clauses, and digresses endlessly in the body of his work, rather than making use of separate footnotes. As his wife later admitted: "So many things came to him out of the storehouse of his mind once the mass of ideas was set in motion, that many times they could not be readily forced into a lucid sentence structure."

It is useless to "simplify" Weber's constructions, since in the process much of the original meaning is lost. It is, however, possible and even necessary to translate certain terms with an ear to a more familiar modern usage. Thus certain terms that, though not common usage at the time of Weber's writing, have since become part of the lingua franca of the social sciences, were used to designate the meaning of Weber's original language. For example, throughout this translation the term behavior (or conduct) has been used to render *handeln* since it would appear to be preposterous in the age of the behaviorist sciences to acquaint the newcomer to Weber with any other term. Undoubtedly those who continue to pursue their studies of Weber will notice that this term as well as others have received different treatment from various translators. This should merely emphasize however the excrutiating nature of the task of obtaining a literal rendering of Weber's work.

In conclusion it is necessary to state that Weber's influence on the development of social sciences in the United States can hardly be overestimated. Much of this is evident in the important scientific work of such scholars as Talcott Parsons, Hans Morgenthau, C. Wright Mills or R. H. Tawney and even in the popularizations of such men as Vance Packard and W. H. White. Weber's work will remain memorable for his groundbreaking explorations in the fields of sociology, history and politics, and for its general contribution to the widening of the horizons of modern scholarship. In this respect his opening up of intellectual virgin territory can be compared to a methodological consciousness reminiscent of Galileo. What Galileo did for the natural sciences Weber has in effect done for the social sciences: He completed the final link to pure science, both substantively and methodologically. He raised social science in the United States and elsewhere in the Western world from the mire of opinions and opinionated talk, documentation of the obvious and/or mystical speculations to the level of real research and scholarship. It was not without reason that Weber could still complain bitterly that, during his lifetime at least, "most of what goes by the name of sociology today is fraud." That this is no longer true is due first and foremost to Max Weber and his disciples.

A man will always be best known by the opinions held by his friends and enemies, and Max Weber is no exception. Karl Jaspers, one of the great living German scholars and Weber's admirer, said of him that he was reason himself. Eric Voegelin, whose theoretical position is diametrically opposed to that of Weber (hardly a more biting criticism of Weber can be found anywhere than in Voegelin's *The New Science of Politics* [Chicago, 1952]), still calls him "A thinker . . . who wanted clarity about the world in which he passionately participated; [who] was headed again on the road toward essence." Voegelin goes on to speak of Weber, despite fundamental disagreements, as a great teacher, the grandeur of whose work arouses admiration and is indeed "awe-inspiring." And it appears only fitting to conclude this brief profile of Max Weber with the judgment of another unrelenting opponent of his hypotheses, Professor Leo Strauss of the University of Chicago, who said of Weber, "Whatever may have been his errors, he is the greatest social scientist of our century."

H. P. SECHER

Western Reserve University

PREFATORY NOTE

The methodology on which these introductory concepts are based may appear abstract, and therefore somewhat remote from reality. Yet such methodological considerations cannot very well be dispensed with, though no claim is being made to originality; instead their aim is to formulate a more usable as well as more correct terminology that will convey clearly the actual meaning of any empirical social science in its concern with similar concepts. This would be true even where new and unfamiliar terms are employed. It may, for that reason, occasionally sound rather pedantic. Compared with the essay in Logos IV (1913, p. 253ff. Reprinted in *Ges. Aufs. z. Wissenschaftslehre,* 2nd ed., p. 427ff), however, the terminology has been simplified wherever possible and therefore has undergone frequent changes in order to render it more easily understandable. Since the requirement for greater simplification cannot always be reconciled with that for precise conceptualization, the latter must occasionally yield to the former.

Concerning the concept of "understanding," compare the *Allgemeine Psychopathologie* by K. Jaspers, as well as some observations by H. Rickert in the 2nd Edition of *Grenzen der naturwissenschaftlichen Begriffsbildung,* (1913, p. 514-523), and especially by Simmel in his *Problemen der Geschichtsphilosophie.* As on some previous occasions, I refer you methodologically to the example of F. Gottl, whose book *Die Herr-*

schaft des Wortes is, to be sure, extremely difficult to understand and appears not to have been completely reasoned out; also pertinent, substantively, is the very fine work by F. Toennies, *Gemeinschaft und Gesellschaft*. Further, there is the strongly misleading work by R. Staemmler, *Wirtschaft und Recht nach der materialistischen Geschichtsauffassung*, together with my critical analysis of it in *Archiv f. Sozialwissensch.* XXIV 1907. (Reprinted in *Ges. Aufs. z. Wissenschaftslehre*, 2nd Ed. p. 291ff). This critical analysis already contained some of the basic formulations of what is about to follow. I depart from Simmel's methodology (in his *Soziologie* and in his *Philos. d. Geldes*) by distinguishing wherever feasible the essentially subjective from the objectively valid meaning; these two terms are not sufficiently differentiated by Simmel but are used by him often deliberately so as to suggest their interchangeability.

MAX WEBER

BASIC CONCEPTS IN SOCIOLOGY

(Paragraph 1

ON THE CONCEPT OF SOCIOLOGY
AND THE "MEANING" OF SOCIAL CONDUCT

The term "sociology" is open to many different interpretations. In the context used here it shall mean that science which aims at the interpretative understanding of social behavior in order to gain an explanation of its causes, its course, and its effects. It will be called human "behavior" only in so far as the person or persons involved engage in some subjectively meaningful action. Such behavior may be mental or external; it may consist in action or omission to act. The term "social behavior" will be reserved for activities whose intent is related by the individuals involved to the conduct of others and is oriented accordingly.

A. METHODOLOGICAL FOUNDATIONS

1. "Meaning" is used here in two different senses. First, there is actual conduct by a specific actor in a given historical situation or the rough approximation based on a given quantity of cases involving many actors; and, second, there is the conceptually "ideal type" of subjective meaning attributed to a hypothetical actor in a given type of conduct. In neither sense can it be used as an objectively "valid" or as a metaphysically fathomable "true" meaning. Herein lies the distinction between the behavioral sciences, such as Sociology and History and the orthodox disciplines, such as Jurisprudence, Logic, Ethics, or Esthetics, whose purpose it is to determine the "true" and "valid" meaning of the objects of their analysis.

2. The line between meaningful and merely responsive behavior (i.e., subjectively not meaningful) is extremely fluid. A significant part of all sociologically relevant behavior, principally purely traditional behavior (see below), fluctuates between the two. Meaningful, i.e. subjectively understandable conduct does not figure at all in many cases of psychophysical processes, or, if it does, is recognizable only by the expert; mystical experiences which cannot be adequately communicated in words are never fully understandable for anyone who is not susceptible to such experiences. On the other hand, the ability to perform a similar action is not a precondition to understanding; it is not necessary "to be Caesar in order to understand Caesar." To be able to put one's self in the place of the actor is important for clearness of understanding but not an absolute precondition for meaningful interpretation. Understandable and non-understandable parts of a process are often inextricably intertwined.

3. All interpretation, as does science generally, strives for clarity and verifiable proof. Such proof of understanding will be either of a rational, i.e., logical or mathematical, or of an emotionally emphatic, artistically appreciative, character. Rational proof can be supplied in the sphere of behavior by a clear intellectual grasp of everything within its intended context of meaning. Emphatic proof in the sphere of behavior will be supplied by complete sympathetic emotional participation. Direct and unambiguous intelligibility is rational understanding of the highest order, especially in mathematically and logically related propositions. We understand plainly what it means when anyone uses the proposition $2+2=4$, or the Pythagorean theorem in reasoning or argument, or when a chain of reasoning is logically executed in accordance with accepted ways of thought. In the same way we understand the actions of a person who

tries to achieve a certain goal by choosing appropriate means, if the facts of the situation on the basis of which he makes his choice are familiar to us. Any interpretation of such rationally purposeful action possesses—for an understanding of the means employed—the highest degree of proof. Not with the same accuracy, but still accurate enough for most purposes of explanation, it is possible to understand errors (including problem entanglements) to which we ourselves are susceptible or whose origin can be detected by sympathetic self-analysis. On the other hand, many ultimate *goals* or *values* toward which experience shows that human behavior may be oriented often cannot be understood as such, though it is possible to grasp them intellectually. The more radically they vary from our own ultimate values, the more difficult it is for us to understand them through sympathetic participation. Depending upon the circumstances of a particular case, it must then suffice to achieve only a purely intellectual understanding of such values or, failing that, a simple acceptance of them as given data. As far as is possible, the conduct motivated by these values can then be understood on the basis of whatever opportunities appear to be available for a sympathetic emotional and/or intellectual interpretation at different stages of its development. Here belong many zealous acts of religion or piety which are quite incomprehensible to those not susceptible to such values; as well as the extreme rationalistic fanaticism typical of the exponents of the "rights of man" theories which are abhorrent to those who, for their part, emphatically repudiate them.

As our susceptibility grows, the more readily are we able to experience such true passions as fear, anger, ambition, envy, jealousy, love, enthusiasm, pride, vengeance, pity, devotion and other desires of every kind, as well as the irrational behavior issuing from them. Even when the degree of intensity in which these emotions are found far surpasses our own potentialities for experiential understanding, we can still interpret intellectually their impact on the direction taken by our behavior as well as the choice of means used to implement it. For purposes of systematic scientific analysis it will be convenient to represent all irrational, emotionally conditioned elements of conduct as deviations from a conceptually pure type of goal-oriented behavior. For example, an analysis of a crisis on the stock exchange would be most conveniently attempted in the following manner: First, a determination of how it would have run its course in the absence of irrational factors; second, using the foregoing as a hypothetical premise, the irrational components are then singled out as "deviation" from the norm. In the same way, the determination of the rational course of a political or military campaign needs first to be made in the light of all known circumstances and known goals of the participants. Only then will it be possible to account for the causal significance of irrational factors as deviations from the ideal type.

The construction of a purely rational "goal-oriented" course of conduct, because of its clear understandability and rational unambiguity, serves sociology as an "ideal type". Thus we are aided in our understanding of the way in which actual goal-oriented conduct is influenced by irrational factors of every kind (such as emotion, errors) and which then can be classified as deviations from the original hypothesized behavior.

Only in this respect and because of methodological efficiency can the method of sociology be considered "rationalistic." Naturally, this procedure may not be interpreted as a rationalistic bias on the part of sociology, but simply as a methodological device. Neither can it be considered as evidence of the predominance of rationalism in human existence. To what extent the reality of rationalism does determine conduct is not to be considered here. That there is a danger of rationalistic interpretations in the wrong place will not be denied. Unfortunately, all experience confirms the existence of such a danger.

4. On the other hand, certain "meaningless" (i.e., devoid of subjective meaning) processes and phenomena exist in all sciences of human behavior. They act as stimuli, or effects, and they either encourage or inhibit human conduct. Such "meaningless" behavior should not be confused with inanimate or non-human behavior. Every artifact (e.g., a machine) acquires meaning only to the extent that its production and use will serve to influence human behavior; such meaning may be quite varied in its purposes. But without reference to such meaning the object remains completely unintelligible.

What makes this object intelligible then is its relation to human behavior in its role of either means or end. It is this relationship of which the individual can claim to have awareness and to which his conduct has been oriented. Only in terms of such categories does an understanding of objects of this kind arise.

On the other hand, all processes or conditions remain "meaningless" if they cannot be related to a meaningful purpose; this regardless of whether they are inanimate, human or inhuman. In other words, they are devoid of meaning if they cannot be related to behavior in their role as means or ends, but operate simply as stimuli, either releasing or inhibiting such behavior.

It is possible, for example, to view the bursting of the River Dollart in 1277 as a powerful stimulus to ensuing migratory movements. The process of decaying, indeed the whole organic life cycle—from the helplessness of the infant to that of the old man—obtains its primary sociological moment from the various ways in which human behavior has become conditioned to these facts. Certain psychic or psycho-physical phenomena such as fatigue, discipline, and memory must be viewed as yet another category of facts that are devoid of meaning; also typical states of euphoria caused by certain conditions of self-punishment, or typical variations in reactions of individuals depending on time, precision, and nature. In the last analysis the principle to be adhered to is the same as with other unintelligible phenomena; they provide the source of "data" for both the observer and the participant.

It is altogether possible that in the future research may uncover non-intelligible uniformities under what had appeared to be, until then, distinctly meaningful behavior, though this has hardly been the case so far. For example, differences in inherited biological characteristics (racial) must be accepted by sociology in the same way as are the physiological facts of the need of nutrition or of the effects of senescence on human behavior. Such data would be acceptable only, of course, insofar as statistically conclusive proof could be supplied of their influence on sociologically relevant behavior. The recognition of such causal significance would not change in the least the task of sociology, which is to interpret intelligible human conduct. The result would be merely to introduce at certain points the same unintelligible data that are already present (see above) into the complex of meaningful motivations; such data as, for example, the typical relations existing between the frequency of certain goal-oriented behavior or the extent of its rationality and the cephalic index or skin color or any other physiological inherited characteristic.

5. Understanding may be of two kinds: first, direct empirical

understanding of the meaning of a given act (incl. a verbal utterance). It is in this sense that we "understand" (i.e., directly) the meaning of the proposition that $2x2 = 4$, when we hear or read it. Here we experience direct, rational understanding of an idea. In the same way, we understand a fit of anger as expressed by exclamations, facial expression or irrational movements. This is direct empirical understanding of irrational emotional reactions and it belongs in the same category as the observation of the action of a woodcutter or of somebody who reaches for a doorknob to shut the door or who aims a gun at an animal. This is rational empirical observation of behavior.

Understanding may also be of a second kind, and this is known as explanatory understanding. We are capable of understanding the motives of anyone who states that $2x2 = 4$ (either orally or in writing) precisely at a particular time and under a definite set of circumstances. Such understanding may be gained if the person under observation is engaged in some bookkeeping task or in a scientific demonstration or some other project of which this task is an essential part. This is rationally based understanding of motivation, i.e., the act is seen as part of an intelligible situation. Motivational is added to observational understanding if we know that the aiming of the gun is done for recreation and the chopping of wood for compensation. Or, in the former instance, the act may be done in order to release certain pent-up emotions, in which case the conduct assumes an irrational character, or because the person aiming the gun has been ordered to do so as a member of a firing squad, or he is firing at an enemy (in either case his behavior is again rational) or because he is exercising his desire for revenge (in which case he reverts to irrational behavior). Finally, we understand motivationally a fit of anger, if we know that its immediate cause can be found in jealousy, hurt pride or injured vanity, all of which are emotionally caused and therefore traceable to irrational motives.

In all the above situations the behavior in question can be designated as part of an understandable sequence of emotions. Such understanding can be accepted as true explanation of the actual course of behavior. For a science dealing with the true meaning of behavior, explanation requires: a grasp of the context of meaning within which the actual course of action occurs. In all such cases, even those involving emotional processes, the subjective meaning within the relevant context of its meaning, will be designated 'intended' meaning; thus we move beyond the customary usage which regards as intentional only (rationally-purposive) goal-oriented behavior.

6. To understand means therefore in all these cases: interpretative understanding of a.) concrete individual cases, as for example in historical analysis; b.) average cases, that is, approximate estimates, as in sociological mass analysis; or c.) a pure type of a frequently occurring scientifically formulated construct. Such ideally typical constructs are, for example, the concepts and axioms of pure economic theory. They show how a given type of human behavior would occur, on a strictly rational basis, unaffected by errors or emotional factors, and if, further, it were directed only to a single goal. Actual behavior takes this course only rarely (e.g., on the stock exchange) and then only approximately so as to correspond to the ideal type. (On the purpose of such constructions, see my discussions in *Archiv f. Sozialwissenschaft* vol. XIX, p. 64ff [Reprinted in *Ges. Aufs. z. Wissenschaftslehre*, p. 190ff] and below, sec. 11).

To be sure, every interpretation strives to achieve utmost verifiability. But even the most verifiable interpretation cannot claim the character of being causally valid. It will remain only a particularly plausible hypothesis. Thus what appears to be conscious motivation to the individual involved may only serve to hide the deeper lying motives and repressions that are really at the root of his behavior and in this way invalidating even the most sincere attempts at self-analysis. In such a case it becomes the task of sociology to inquire into the deeper meaning of such motivation and interpret it accurately, even though this motivation has not been fully part of the conscious behavior of the individual in question: it becomes therefore a borderline case of meaningful interpretation.

Again, forms of behavior which appear to the observer to share the same or similar characteristics may be based on a variety of motives on the part of the individual actor. Situations of this kind which appear to share some superficial characteristics must be interpreted quite differently, even if this leads to conflicting analysis. Finally, the individuals involved in any given situation frequently respond to opposing impulses, all of which can be understood by us. We know from experience it is not always possible to estimate even approximately the relative strength of motives and very often we cannot even be certain of our own interpretation. Only the final result of the conflict provides us with a solid basis for judgment. The verification of interpretation by its results, i.e., the decisiveness of the actual course of events, is, as is true of all hypotheses, indispensable. Unfortunately, such verifiable interpretations can be obtained with relative accuracy only in a very few and special cases of the kind suitable for psychological experimentation; or, aiming at a different degree of approximation, through statistically quantifiable data of mass phenomena. For the rest, there remains only the possibility of comparing a maximum number of historical processes or routine phenomena of everyday experience and of similar appearance but differing substantially regarding the motivational factor under investigation. This is the fundamental task of comparative sociology. Unfortunately, there often remains only the uncertain instrument of purely hypothetical experiments, which ignores certain elements in the chain of motivation and leads instead to the construction of a merely probable course of events that might lend itself to causal attribution.

For example, the postulate known as Gresham's Law is a rational interpretation of human conduct within a given context and on the basis of an ideal hypothesis of a purely rational course. To what extent such behavior really follows Gresham's Law can be ascertained only on the basis of statistical information concerning the disappearance of under-valued money, and generally our experience has shown the validity of this law. In this case the data were first accumulated, followed by the formulation of a suitable generalization. But without such a successful interpretation we could not have satisfied our need for true causal understanding. On the other hand, the absence of proof that the action inferred from this behavior occurs with some regularity, would make a law, no matter how much theoretical proof could be obtained, quite valueless for purposes of concrete analysis. In this case the theoretical interpretation of motivation and its empirical verification display considerable conformity and there are a sufficient number of cases to consider proof to have been established satisfactorily.

But to use another illustration, the ingenious theory developed by Eduard Meyers as to the causal significance of the battles of Salamis and Platea for the unique evolution of Greek and hence occidental culture generally (He bases it on symptomatic facts concerning the attitude of the Hellenic oracles and of the prophets toward the Persians) does not submit easily to such proof. Verification can be obtained only by reference to the conduct of the Persians in cases where they were victorious, as for example in Jerusalem, Egypt, and Asia Minor, and even this verification must necessarily remain incomplete in many respects. What provides this hypothesis with such strong support is its striking rational plausibility. Yet in many cases of such highly plausible historical interpretations, what is lacking is the possibility of the kind of proof that was still feasible even in this case. Under such circumstances the interpretation must remain purely hypothetical.

7. "Motivation" as used here refers to a complex of meaning which appears to the individual involved or to the observer to be sufficient reason for his conduct. A *meaningfully adequate level* of understanding refers to a subjective interpretation of a coherent course of behavior whose component parts articulate with each other, within the context of our accustomed modes of thought and feeling, to the point of constituting a "typical" complex of meaning. It is usually called "correct," rather than typical. In contrast, we will consider an interpretation of a sequence of events to be *causally adequate*, if on the basis of past experience it appears probable that it will always occur in the same way.

An example of a meaningfully adequate level of interpretation can be encountered in the correct solution of an arithmetical problem, if it accords with accepted norms of calculation and of reasoning. On the other hand, a causally adequate interpretation of the same phenomenon would concern the statistical probability that, in line with tested empirical generalizations, there would be a correct or incorrect solution of the same

39

problem. Though this would accept prevailing normative standards it would also take into account typical errors or confusions. Causal explanations therefore postulate: a rarely quantifiable but always somehow calculable probability that any certain observable overt or subjective event is either followed or accompanied by another event.

A correct causal interpretation of a concrete course of behavior is achieved when such overt behavior and its motives have both been correctly ascertained and if, at the same time, their relationship has become intelligible in a meaningful way. A correct causal interpretation of a typical course of behavior then can be taken to mean that the process which is claimed to be typical is shown to lend itself to both meaningful and causally adequate interpretation. If no meaning attaches itself to such typical behavior, then regardless of the degree of uniformity or the statistical preciseness of probability, it still remains an incomprehensible statistical probability, whether it deals with an overt or subjective process. On the other hand, even the most perfectly adequate meaning is causally significant from a sociological point of view only if we have proof that in all likelihood the conduct in question normally unfolds in a meaningful way. In order for this to occur there must be determinable some degree of frequency of approximation to an average or an ideal type.

In the present context, statistical uniformities constitute intelligible types of behavior, i.e., sociological generalizations, only when they manifest the understandable subjective meaning of a course of social behavior. Again, only those rational constructs of subjectively intelligible conduct can be considered as sociological types of empirical process if they can be empirically observed with at least a degree of approximation. It is hardly ever the case that the actual likelihood of the occurrence of a given course of behavior will always be directly proportional to the clarity of subjective interpretation. At any rate, only experience can tell whether this will always be true. It is possible, after all, to obtain statistical information of processes that are devoid of meaning as well as of those with meaning: the amount of rainfall, the death rate, phenomena of fatigue, and the productivity of machines are good examples of the former, while crime rates, occupational distributions, price statistics, and crop acreage statistics are examples of the latter; and only in these latter examples is it possible to speak of sociological statistics. Of course there are many cases, as in crop statistics, which contain both kinds of meaning.

8. Processes and uniformities which because of their unintelligibility are not designated here as sociological phenomena or uniformities are not necessarily less important on that account. This is true also for sociology in our present context, which implies a restriction to subjectively understandable phenomena and which no one is forced to accept. They are simply moved into a different category from that of meaningful behavior, which is methodologically unavoidable: thus they become conditions, stimuli, inhibiting or encouraging the environment in which behavior occurs.

9. "Behavior" in the sense of subjectively intelligible orientation of behavior exists only as the behavior of one or more individual persons. For other analytical purposes it may be useful and even necessary to look at the individual as a collection of cells or a bundle of bio-chemical reactions, or conceive of his psyche as composed of a number of variously defined elements. This would certainly yield valuable insight into causal relationships. Yet we do not really understand subjectively the

behavior of these elements as expressed in these uniformities. We do not even understand it with psychic elements: the more scientifically exact their definition, the less do we understand them; this never leads to interpretation in terms of subjective meaning. But for both sociology and history the real object for analysis should be the deeper meaning of certain behavior. The behavior of certain physiological entities, e.g., cells, or of any sort of psychic elements, may at least be observed in principle in such a way as to lead to the creation of certain postulates applicable to individually uniform phenomena. But the subjective understanding of behavior recognizes such facts and uniformities as well as any others not capable of subjective interpretation: for example, of physical, astronomical, geological, meteorological, geographical, botanical, zoological, anatomical data as well as of such data relating to psychopathology which are devoid of subjective meaning or those of the scientific conditions giving rise to technological progress.

For still other purposes of analyses, e.g., legal or practical ends, it may be convenient and even unavoidable to treat social groups, such as the state, cooperative associations, business corporations, and foundations as if they were individual persons with rights and duties and as the executors of legally significant conduct. But for sociologically meaningful interpretations such organizations are merely the result of distinct behavior of individual persons, since they alone can engage as agents in any kind of meaningful behavior. Nevertheless, the sociologist for his purposes can hardly ignore such concepts of collectivity that derive from different vantage points. For the subjective interpretation of behavior is related to such concepts in at least three different ways.

a.) Such interpretation is frequently forced to work with

similar (even identical) concepts in order to establish a meaningful terminology generally. Both legal as well as lay terminology defines the *state* as a legal concept and a phenomenon of social behavior to which its legal rules are relevant. But for sociological purposes the term "state" does not consist necessarily or even primarily of legally relevant components. In any case, sociology does not recognize a "behaving" (*acting*) collective personality. When sociology uses the terms "state," "nation," "corporation," "family," "army division" or similarly collective concepts, it does so merely to focus on a certain kind of development of alternative modes of social behavior by individual persons. Thus the legal terminology, which is used because of its precision and usage, obtains here a completely different meaning.

b.) The interpretation of behavior also has to take into account a most important vital fact: these collective concepts derived from legal, common sense or any other technical ideas, are meaningful to individuals either because they exist at least partially or because they represent something with a normative authority. This is true not only of judges and of bureaucrats but of the public at large as well. Individuals orient their conduct to them and in this way they very often exercise a very real, dominating causal influence on the course of behavior of these individuals. Especially is this true where these concepts are part of a recognized positive or negative pattern. The modern *state* represents to a not inconsiderable degree a complex of concerted action on the part of individual persons as well, because many people act in the belief that it exists or should exist in precisely this way to provide legal validity for the issuance of its orders. This will be discussed further below. Though it would be possible for sociological terminology to eliminate these concepts from common usage as being too pedantic and all-inclusive and substitute new terms, it would be, at least in the present context, quite out of the question.

c.) There is finally the method of the so-called organic school of sociology, of which Schaeffle's brilliant work, *Bau und Leben des sozialen Koerpers*, represents a classical example. This school attempts to explain social interaction by using as its premise the "whole" (e.g., economics) to which the individual's behavior is related and then interpreted. This process is similar to the way in which a physiologist would analyze the role of a bodily organ within the community of organisms, i.e., how it contributes toward the survival of the rest of the organism. In this context there may be recalled the famous dictum of a physiologist during a seminar: "Paragraph X:" he said, "the Spleen. Gentlemen we know nothing about the spleen. So much for the spleen." Of course, a great deal was "known" about the spleen, such as position, size, shape, etc.; only its "functions" could not be ascertained and this absence of knowledge he characterized as ignorance. To what extent other disciplines regard this manner of functional analysis of the parts of a whole as definitive need not be discussed here; but it is well-known that bio-chemical and bio-physical forms of analysis of the organism are not exhausted with such a functional approach.

For purposes of sociological analysis such an approach is of importance because it serves first as a convenient point of departure for purposes of demonstration, as well as for provisional orientation. In this form it may be highly useful and even necessary—but at the same time, if its empirical value is overestimated, or if it is simply overconceptualized, the advantages of such an approach are lost. Secondly, it may be the only way under certain circumstances of determining just what processes of social behavior are necessary for our understanding in order to explain a particular phenomenon. It is at this stage that the real task of sociology, as we understand it, begins.

In the case of social collectivities we are especially in a position to create something that goes beyond the demonstration of the functional relationships and uniformities usually found in physical or biological organisms. Unlike the process in the natural sciences, we can here obtain a subjective interpretation of the behavior of the individuals directly involved. This is so because the natural sciences are limited to the formulation of causal uniformities in objects and events and to the explanation of individual facts by applying them. We do not really "understand" the behavior of cells but merely recognize their functional relationship, on the basis of which we then introduce a generalization. This additional success of explanation by interpretative understanding, rather than by mere empirical observation, is of course obtained at a price, which is the essentially hypothetical and fragmentary character of the results achieved in this manner. Still, it is precisely this kind of subjective understanding which provides sociological analysis with its distinct character.

This is not the place to discuss also the extent to which the behavior of animals becomes subjectively understandable to us or our behavior to them; such understanding is highly uncertain and its application most problematical. But insofar as such understanding exists, it would be conceivable to formulate a sociology of the relations of man to animals, both domestic and wild. It is true, after all, that many animals "understand" orders, wrath, love, aggressiveness and react to them not merely instinctively and mechanically but consciously meaningful and on the basis of previous experience. Our own ability to identify ourselves with the behavior of primitive peoples is hardly likely to be any better. But neither do we have any reliable means of determining the subjective state of mind of any animal or if we do, it is at best very unsatisfactory.

The problems of animal psychology are known for being interesting as well as difficult. It is also known that there are animal social organizations of many kinds: monogamous and polygamous "families," herds, flocks, and even "states" with a functional division of labor. The extent of functional differentiation of these animal societies by no means parallels that of the organic or morphological differentiation of individual members of the species. For example, the functional differentiation found among termites, and therefore that of the products of their social organization, is far more advanced than that found among the ants and bees. Here it may well be that the observer must be satisfied with achieving a purely functional analysis. Such an analysis would enable him to study the means which the species regards as indispensable for its survival: nutrition, defense, reproduction and reconstruction, and to identify those animals charged with the execution of these and other functions, i.e., kings and queens, workers, soldiers, drones, propagators, substitute queens, etc. Anything beyond that would remain for a long time merely speculation or investigations of the extent to which heredity on the one hand and environment on the other, would be involved in the development of these "social" proclivities. This was particularly true of the controversies between Goette and Weisman. Weisman's concept of the omnipotence of natural selection was based largely on wholly nonempirical deductions. Still, all serious authorities are agreed that the reduction to a functional level of analysis is simply a necessity and will, it is hoped, be of a purely temporary character.

(Compare, for example, on the state of knowledge of the termites, the study by Escherich, 1909). We would like to know not only the significance of the functions of these many differentiated types for survival, but also how, for example, the theory of the inheritance of acquired characteristics—or its opposite—bears on the problem of explaining the origins of these differentiations, as well as the influence of different variants on that theory. In addition, it would be well to know first what factors are decisive for the original differentiation of specialized types from the still neutral undifferentiated species type; second, what causes the individual once it is differentiated to act in a manner calculated to bring about the survival of the differentiated group. Wherever some progress has been made in the research on these problems, it occurred through experimental demonstration of the probability or possibility regarding the role of chemical stimuli or physiological processes such as nutritional habits, effects of parasitic castration, etc., in the case of individual organisms. How far there is even the ghost of a chance to make the existence of "psychological" (i.e., subjective) or meaningful orientation experimentally possible, even the expert would hardly venture to guess.

A verifiable presentation of the psyche of these social animals lending itself to meaningful understanding would appear to be attainable even as an ideal goal only within very narrow limits. At any rate, we cannot expect to obtain from this source any real contribution to the understanding of human social behavior. On the contrary—in the field of animal psychology human analogy will and ought to be used cautiously. We may expect, however, that some day such biological analogies will be useful in suggesting significant new approaches. For example, they may throw light on the question of how in the early stages of human social differentiation the impact of mechanical and instinctive factors must be calculated in, as compared to that of those factors which are accessible to subjective interpretation generally and, more specifically, to that of consciously rational behavior. Interpretative sociology will have to be made to recognize that for early human development it is the impact of the first set of factors which is of decisive importance and that even in the later stages recognition must be had of their continuous interaction with others.

Traditional behavior and especially charismatic behavior often carry the seeds of psychic contagion and thereby act as transmission belts for many evolutionary stimuli of the social process. Such types of behavior are closely related to phenomena that can be understood either solely in biological terms or are subject to incomplete interpretation in terms of subjective motives, fusing almost imperceptibly into the biological. None of this relieves sociology of the obligation to accomplish, even within such narrow limits, what only it alone can do.

The various works by Othman Spann are rich in suggestive ideas along these lines, though frequently he too errs on the side of pure value judgments that are not part of a true empirical investigation. Nevertheless, he is undoubtedly right in his emphasis on the importance of a functional point of view for the preliminary investigation of a social problem; this is what he calls the "universalist method."

What we need to know primarily is what kind of behavior is functional in terms of survival and, above all, necessary for the continuation of cultural uniqueness and the continuity of the corresponding types of social behavior, before we can inquire into its origins and motivation. First, we need to know what a king, an official, an entrepreneur, a procurer, a magician, a producer does: i.e., what kind of behavior is typical and important enough to justify his being classified in any of these categories and is therefore relevant to analysis prior to the beginning of such analysis. (This is what H. Rickert means by value judgment.) But it is only such analysis which achieves understanding of the behavior of typically differentiated human (and only human) individuals and therefore is to be considered the specific function of sociology.

It is in any case a tremendous misunderstanding to assume that an individualistic methodology presupposes also an individualistic system of values. This assumption is as faulty as the related one of confusing the relatively unavoidable tendency of social concepts to acquire a rational character with the belief that rational motives always predominate or that rationalism can be positively evaluated.

Even a socialist economy would be individualistic for purposes of sociological analysis. That is, it must be understood on the basis of individual behavior—for example that of the functionaries who run it; and this would be equally true in the case of a free market system which is analyzed in terms of the theory of marginal utility, though it might be possible to find a more suitable but still similar method. Truly empirical sociological investigation begins only with the question, what did and still does motivate the individual functionaries and members of the community to conduct themselves in such a way as to bring about the creation of this "community" and to insure its continuation? Any formal functional analysis that uses the 'whole' as its point of departure can accomplish only preliminary preparations for further investigation; its utility and indispensabilty is, if it is properly applied, of course incontestable.

10. The various sociological generalizations which it is cus-

tomary to identify as "scientific laws," as for example, Gresham's Law, are in fact typical probabilities confirmed by observation. The assumption is that under certain given conditions a projected course of action will occur which will be intelligible in terms of typical motives and of the typical subjective intentions of those engaged in a certain behavior. These generalizations are both understandable and definitive to the highest degree insofar as the typically observed course of behavior can be understood in terms of the purely rational pursuit of a goal, or where for reasons of methodological convenience such a theoretical type can be heuristically employed; in such cases the relationship between means and ends is clearly understood empirically, especially where the choice of means was "inevitable." In such an instance it can be legitimately stated that insofar as the conduct was strictly goal-oriented it could not have taken any other direction. The reasons would be primarily technical, since, given the clearly defined ends, no other means were available to the individuals engaged in such behavior. Such a case shows emphatically how mistaken it is to regard any kind of psychology as the ultimate foundation of the sociological interpretation of human behavior. To be sure, everybody appears today to have his own interpretation of psychology. Certain definite methodological purposes justify a treatment of certain types of process which attempts to follow the procedures of the natural sciences, separating the "physical" from the "psychic" phenomena in a manner quite alien to the disciplines concerned with human behavior.

The results of psychological investigation which employs the methods of the natural sciences in any number of possible ways may, naturally, just like those of any other science, have, within certain limits, great significance for sociological problems; and indeed this has happened frequently. However, such use of psychological data must be distinguished from any investigation of human behavior in terms of its subjective meaning. Consequently, sociology does not bear any closer logical relationship to psychology than to any other science. The fault here lies with a concept of "psychic" which regards everything non-physical as *ipso facto* psychic; yet the real meaning of the solution of a mathematical problem by a person is not a "psychic" process: the rational deliberations by an individual, whether or not the results of a certain contemplated course of conduct will promote certain specific interests, together with the corresponding decision, do not become one iota more intelligible on the basis of psychological considerations. Yet it is precisely such rational assumptions on which rest most of the laws of sociology as well as of economics. On the other hand, in explaining irrational conduct sociologically, interpretive psychology (i.e., the form which uses subjective understanding) undoubtedly can be of decisive value. But this does not change the fundamental methodological situation.

11. The premise has been repeatedly stated that the science of sociology attempts to formulate typological concepts and generalized uniformities of empirical process. This is in contrast to history, which strives for the causal analysis and explanation of culturally significant behavior of individuals, institutions and of certain personalities. The data which underlie the conceptualizations of sociology consist essentially, though not exclusively, of the same relevant processes of behavior that are dealt with by historians. Its concepts and generalizations are fashioned on the premise that it can claim to make a contribution to the causal explanation of some historically and culturally important phenomenon. As is true of any other generalizing

science, the abstract character of sociological concepts is responsible for the relative absence of concrete content when compared with actual historical reality. But what sociology offers instead is an increased precision of concepts. Such greater precision is obtained by striving for the highest possible degree of adequacy on the level of meaning which is in accordance with the sociological conceptualization put forward above. It has been repeatedly stressed that this aim can be realized to a particularly high degree in the case of concepts and generalizations which formulate—goal-oriented or value-related—rational processes. But sociology tries to encompass also various irrational phenomena (i.e. mystic, prophetic, pneumatic, as well as affectual), in terms of theoretical concepts that are adequate on the level of meaning. In all cases, rational as well as irrational, sociology distances itself from reality, yet serves to understand it, in that it shows with what degree of approximation a concrete historical phenomenon can be subsumed under any of these concepts.

For example, the same historical phenomenon may have feudal, patrimonial, historical and charismatic aspects. To provide these terms with the necessary precision, sociology must design "pure" ("ideal") types of corresponding forms of human behavior, which in each case involve the highest possible degree of logical integration because of their complete adequacy on the level of meaning. But for the very reason that this is so, it is hardly ever, if at all, probable that a real phenomenon can be found which corresponds exactly to one of these ideally constructed types. The situation is similar to the calculation of a physical reaction on the basis of an absolute vacuum. Only on the basis of such ideal types is theoretical analysis possible in the field of sociology. It is understood of course that, in addition, it is convenient for the sociologist to employ occasionally average types of an empirical-statistical character; these concepts do not require methodological discussion at this point. But when sociology refers to typical cases it must always be understood, unless stated otherwise, that the term means ideal types, be they rational or irrational (in economic theory it is always the former), but that they are, in any case, always constructed with a view to adequacy on the level of meaning.

It is necessary to recognize that in the area of sociology, averages, and therefore average types, can be formulated with greater precision only where it is a matter of qualitatively equal behavior but differing merely in degrees. Such instances do occur, but in most cases of the kind of behavior that is relevant to history or sociology the motives influencing it are qualitatively heterogeneous, none of which can be considered average in the true sense. Those ideal types of social behavior that are encountered in economic theory are "unrealistic" or abstract to the extent that they inquire only into what would happen during a given course of behavior, provided it were purely rational and oriented toward economic ends alone. Such an approach, however, is helpful in the understanding of behavior that is not solely economically determined but is at least influenced by traditional restraints, emotions, errors, and the intrusion of other non-economic factors. This may happen in two ways: First, through an analysis of the economically determining factor together with other factors in a single case or in a number of average cases; or, secondly, the analysis of non-economic factors may be facilitated by emphasizing the discrepancy between the actual course of events and the ideal type. Thus the construction of an ideal type of unworldly attitude toward existence, engendered by mystical influences, would be a similar process of analyzing its consequences for the individual's relation to ordinary life (e.g., to politics or economics). The more distinct and precise the construction of the ideal type, the greater its abstract or unrealistic nature and the better is it able to perform its methodological functions in formulating the clarification of terminology, of classification, and of hypotheses.

In the attribution of concrete causal explanation of individual events, the historical method is essentially the same. For example, an attempt to explain the campaign of 1866 must necessarily involve a reconstruction of how Moltke and Benedek would have acted had they possessed full insight not only into their own situation but into that of their opponent as well. Only then is it possible to make comparisons with the actual course of events and formulate a causal explanation of observed deviations which can be attributed to such factors as misinformation, strategical errors, logical fallacies, personalities or non-strategic considerations. Thus there is latent here, too, an ideal typical construction of rational action.

Yet the ideal-typical constructs of sociology derive their character not only from the objective point of view but also from their application to subjective processes. For the most part, real behavior proceeds at the subconscious or inarticulate conscious level of its subjective meaning. The person behaving in a certain way "feels" this vaguely, rather than being explicitly aware of the source of his behavior. Mostly his behavior is governed by habit or instinct. Only occasionally, and in the uniform behavior of great masses often only in the case of a few individuals, is the subjective meaning of such behavior, be it rational or irrational, raised to the level of true consciousness. Really effective, that is, truly conscious and clearly meaningful behavior, is in reality always a marginal case. Every historical and sociological investigation engaged in the analysis of empirical facts, has to take this into consideration. But this difficulty need not prevent the researcher from formulating concepts through the classification of possible types of subjective meaning; that is, as if behavior actually occurred on the basis of clearly self-conscious meaning. The resulting divergence from concrete facts must be kept continually in view, whenever it is a question of this level of concreteness, and it must be carefully studied with reference both to degree and kind. Methodologically, one has frequently only the alternative of choosing between terms that are unclear and those that are clear; the latter may be abstract ideal types but are for that very reason scientifically preferable. (On all these topics see *Archiv fuer Sozialwissenschaft*, vol. XIX, op. cit. See above, sec. 6.)

B. THE CONCEPT OF SOCIAL CONDUCT

1. Social conduct (including both omission or acquiescence) may be oriented to the past, present, or future conduct of others. Thus it may be caused by feelings of revenge for past wrongs, defense against present dangers or against future attacks. The "others" may be known or unknown individuals or they may constitute an indefinite quantity. For example, "money" is a medium of exchange which the individual accepts in payment because his conduct is oriented in the expectation that numerous but unknown and undetermined "others" will on their part, sometime in the future, accept it as a means of exchange.

2. Not every kind of conduct, even manifestly formal conduct, is "social" in the sense of the present discussion. Formal conduct is non-social if it is oriented exclusively to the behavior of inanimate objects. Subjective attitudes are to be

thought of as social behavior only if they are oriented to the behavior of others. Religious behavior is not social if it remains simply a matter of contemplation or of solitary prayer, etc. The economic activity of an individual is only social if and only insofar as it concerns also the behavior of third persons. Generally speaking, in formal terms it becomes social only insofar as it reflects the extent to which others respect one person's actual control over economic goods. More concretely, it is social if, for example, in relation to a person's own consumption the future wants of others are taken into account and therefore determine the persons own "savings."

3. Not every type of contact between human beings is of a social character, but only where the individual's conduct is meaningfully oriented toward that of others. Thus a collision of two cyclists is merely an isolated event comparable to a natural catastrophe. On the other hand, any attempt by any one of them to avoid hitting the other, with ensuing insults, a brawl or even a peaceful discussion, would constitute a form of "social behavior."

4. Nor is social conduct identical with a) the uniform conduct of many persons, or b) the conduct influenced by other persons. If, for example, at the start of a rainfall a number of persons on the street unfold their umbrellas at the same time, such conduct is normally not oriented to that of others, but simply a similar reaction by all to protect themselves against the rain. It is also well known that the conduct of an individual can be strongly influenced by the mere fact that he is a member of a crowd confined within a limited space. This is the subject of "crowd psychology" research of the type engaged in by Le Bon, and it is known as "crowd-conditioned" behavior. Again, it is possible for large, though widely dispersed, numbers to react

simultaneously or successively to a source of influence which acts similarly on all individuals, as is done, for instance, by the press; the behavior of the individual is in this manner influenced by his membership in the crowd and his awareness of such membership. As a matter of fact, certain types of reaction are only made possible by the mere fact that the individual behaves as part of a crowd, though others are merely made more difficult under such conditions. Consequently it is possible that a particular event or mode of human behavior can give rise to emotions of the most diverse kinds—humor, wrath, enthusiasm, despair or passion—in a crowd situation, which would not happen at all or not nearly so readily if the individual were by himself; this need not necessarily constitute a meaningful relation between the individual's behavior and the fact that he is a member of a crowd. Such conduct, which is merely the result of reactions by the individual to the crowd, is not "social" conduct in the sense used here, especially since there is no orientation of this conduct that can be considered adequate at the level of meaning. Such differences are necessarily highly flexible. For example, not only the demagogue but also his mass audience may be affected in varying degrees by each other's conduct; and such a relationship may lend itself to various interpretations.

Furthermore, mere "imitation" of the conduct of others—correctly emphasized by G. Tarde—will not be considered specifically as "social conduct," if it is simply reactive and not meaningfully oriented toward the individual so imitated. Again, the line of demarcation is extremely flexible, which makes its determination increasingly difficult. The mere fact, however, that someone uses a purposeful scheme which he has seen used by others, does not constitute, in the present sense, social behavior. Behavior such as this is not oriented to that of other persons, but the individual has learned through the observation of others of the existence of certain objective facts and it is to these that his conduct is oriented. His conduct is then causally determined by the behavior of others, but not meaningfully so. On the other hand, if, for example, the conduct of others is imitated because it is the "fashion" or is "tradition" or a "standard" or provides social prestige, or on similar grounds, then it is meaningfully oriented either to the behavior of these being imitated or of third persons or of both. Between these types of imitation there are, of course, all sorts of borderline cases.

Both phenomena, that of the behavior of crowds as well as that of imitation, are fluid concepts on the borderline of social behavior; the same is true of traditionalist types of social behavior of the kind discussed in paragraph 2. The reason for such flexibility in these and similar cases can be found in the fact that the orientation to the behavior of others and the meaning of the individual's own conduct are not always capable of concise determination; and frequently are, indeed, quite unconscious and rarely fully self-conscious. Mere "influence" and meaningful "orientation" are for that reason alone not always capable of empirical distinction. But conceptually it is essential to differentiate between them, even though mere "reactive" imitation has at least the same sociological importance as does the type which constitutes social behavior in the strict sense. Thus sociology is not concerned solely with "social behavior," but such behavior provides (at least for the sociology being developed here) its central subject matter and may be said to be its constituent part as a science. But this does not imply any judgment on the comparative importance of this and other factors.

CHARACTERISTIC FORMS OF SOCIAL CONDUCT

Like any other form of conduct, social conduct may be determined in any one of the following four ways. *First:* It may be classified rationally and oriented toward a goal. In this instance the classification is based on the expectation that objects in the external situation or other human individuals will behave in a certain way, and by the use of such expectations as "conditions" or "means" for the successful achievement of the individual's own rationally chosen goals. Such a case will be called *goal-oriented* conduct. *Second:* Social conduct may be classified by the conscious belief in the absolute worth of the conduct, as such, independent of any ulterior motive and measured by some such standard as ethics, esthetics or religion. Such a case of rational orientation toward an absolute value will be called *value-related* conduct. *Third:* Social conduct may be classified affectually, especially emotionally, the result of a special configuration of feelings and emotions on the part of the individual. *Fourth:* Social conduct may be classified traditionally, having been accustomed to by long practice.

1. Strictly traditionalist behavior—just as the reactive type of imitation discussed above (see par. 1) lies altogether on the borderline and sometimes even crosses what can be called meaningfully oriented conduct. Frequently it is simply a dull reaction—almost automatic—to accustomed stimuli that have led behavior repeatedly along a routine course. The greater part of all routine duties performed habitually by people every day

is of this type; consequently it is not just as a marginal case that it belongs in this classification but also, as will be shown later, because its attachment to what are accustomed forms can be upheld with varying degrees of self-consciousness and in a variety of senses: in that case the type may approach that of number two (value-relatedness).

2. Strictly affectual behavior also straddles the line of what may be considered "meaningfully" oriented, and frequently it, too, crosses the line; for instance, it may be an uninhibited reaction to some extraordinary stimulus. It is a case of sublimation when affectually conditioned behavior issues in the form of conscious release of emotional tensions. When this happens, it is usually, though not always, well on its way either toward value-related or goal-oriented rational conduct or both.

3. Value-related conduct is distinguished from affectual conduct by its conscious formulation of the ultimate values governing such conduct and its consistent planned orientation to these values. At the same time these two types share in the fact that the meaning of the conduct does not lie in the achievement of some goal ulterior to it, but in engaging in the specific type of behavior for its own sake. Affectually determined behavior is the kind which demands the immediate satisfaction of an impulse, regardless of how sublime or sordid it may be, in order to obtain revenge, sensual gratification, complete surrender to a person or ideal, blissful contemplation, or finally to release emotional tensions.

Examples of pure value-related conduct would be the behavior of persons who, regardless of the consequences, conduct themselves in such a way as to put into practice their convictions of what appears to them to be required by duty, honor, beauty, religiosity, piety or the importance of a "cause," no matter what its goal. Within our terminology such value-related behavior is always pursuant to commands or demands whose fulfilment are believed by the person engaging in it to constitute an obligation for him. Only insofar as human conduct is oriented exclusively toward such unconditional demands—and this is true to a very modest degree—will it be considered as "value-related," i.e., oriented toward absolute values. It will be seen that this type of conduct is important enough to justify its being singled out as a special type; though it should be noted that no attempt is made here to formulate in any way an exhaustive classification of certain types of behavior.

4. Rational conduct is of the goal-oriented kind when it is engaged in with due consideration for ends, means, and secondary effects; such conduct must also weigh alternate choices, as well as the relations of the end to other possible uses of the means and, finally, the relative importance of different possible ends. The classification of conduct either in affectual or traditional terms is thus incompatible with this type. The decision between competing and conflicting ends and results may in turn be determined by a consideration of absolute values: in that case, such conduct is goal-oriented only in respect to the choice of means. Or, the person engaged in such conduct may, rather than decide between conflicting or competing ends in terms of value-related orientation, merely take them as given subjective wants and arrange them on a scale in order of priority. He may then orient his conduct according to this scale in such a way that it conforms as far as possible to the order of priority as prescribed by the principle of "marginal utility."

This value-oriented conduct can be variously related to goal-oriented conduct. From the point of view of the latter, however, value-orientation acquires more irrationality the more ab solute it becomes. For, the more unconditionally the individual devotes himself to such value for its own sake—be it because of sentiment, beauty, absolute kindness, or devotion to duty—the less is there any thought of the consequences of such devotion. Absolute goal-oriented conduct—i.e., pure expediency, without any reference to basic values—is essentially only a constructive exception.

5. Rarely is conduct, especially social conduct, oriented only in one or the other of these ways. Nor does this represent an exhaustive classification of the types of conduct now existing; it is meant merely to arrive at certain conceptually pure forms of sociologically important types, to which social conduct is more or less closely approximated, or as is much more usual, which constitute the elements joining to make it up. Only its future success can justify the usefulness of this classification for the purposes of our investigation.

THE CONCEPT OF SOCIAL RELATIONSHIP

The term "social relationship" will be used to designate the situation where two or more persons are engaged in conduct wherein each takes account of the behavior of the other in a meaningful way and is therefore oriented in these terms. The social relationship thus *consists* entirely of the *probability* that individuals will behave in some meaningfully determinable way. It is completely irrelevant why such a probability exists, but where it does there can be found a social relationship.

1. A defining criterion, therefore, demands at least a minimum of mutual orientation of the conduct of each to that of the other. Its content may be most varied: conflict, hostility, sexual attraction, friendship, loyalty or market exchange; it may involve the "fulfilment" or "evasion" or "severance" of an agreement; economic, erotic, or any other form of "competition"; a sharing of occupations or membership in the same class or nation. In the latter cases, mere group membership may not constitute social conduct, as will be discussed later. Furthermore, the definition does not inform as to the degree of solidarity, or its opposite, prevailing among those engaged in this conduct.

2. It is always a case, if used in this context, of the meaning imputed to those individuals involved in a given concrete situation, either on the average or in a theoretically constructed pure type—but it is never a case of normatively "correct" or metaphysically "true" meaning. The social relationship con-

sists even in the case of such "social organizations" as a "state," "church," "association" or "marriage," in the fact that there has existed, exists, or will exist, a probable conduct in some definite way appropriate to this meaning. It is necessary to emphasize this in order to avoid the "reification" of these concepts, i.e., their degeneration into empty conceptualizations.

Thus a "state" loses its sociological significance, as soon as it is probable that it ceases to manifest any kind of meaningfully oriented social behavior. Such probability may be very high or it may be insignificant. But in any case it is only in the sense and degree in which it does exist or can be estimated to exist that the corresponding relationship exists. Otherwise no other meaning can be given to the phrase that a given "state" exists or has ceased to exist.

3. All parties who are mutually oriented in a given social relationship do not necessarily manifest the *same* subjective meaning about it, i.e., there need not be any "reciprocity." "Friendship", "love", "loyalty", "contractual trust", "nationalism", on the one side, may well be faced with an entirely different attitude on the other. To the parties involved, their conduct merely shows various forms and meanings, and the social relationship is simply "asymmetrical." Nevertheless, they may be mutually oriented in so far as one party presumes a particular attitude toward himself on the part of the other and orients his own conduct accordingly. Regardless of whether or not he is mistaken in his expectations, this can, and usually will, result in a certain course of conduct and will have consequences for the form of the relationship. Objectively speaking, a "symmetrical" relationship exists only if in their expectations of this relationship it means the same to all parties involved. For example, the actual attitude of a child to its father may be at least ap-

proximately that which the father, on the whole, has come to expect. A social relationship in which the attitudes are completely and fully oriented toward each other is really a marginal case. According to our terminology, the absence of reciprocity will exclude the existence of a social relationship only if such mutual orientation is really lacking in the behavior of the parties. Here as elsewhere, all sorts of transitional cases are the rule rather than the exception.

4. A social relationship can be of a transitory nature or of varying degrees of permanence. That is, it can be of such a kind that there is a probability of the repeated *recurrence* of the behavior which corresponds to its subjective meaning and is therefore expected because it is in consequence of such meaning. But in order to avoid giving false impressions, it bears repetition to remember that it is *only* the existence of the *probability* that, corresponding to a given subjective meaning complex, a certain type of behavior will take place, which constitutes the *existence* of the social relationship. Thus, that "friendship" or "state" exists or has existed means only this: that in the judgment of *us*, the *observers*, there is or has been the *probability* that, given certain kinds of known subjective attitudes of certain individuals, there will result, *on the average*, a certain specific type of conduct, and nothing else (compare above, No. 2). The unavoidable alternative, from the legal point of view: whether or not a rule of law is endowed with legal validity and a legal relationship therefore can be assumed to exist, such a simple alternative is not relevant to sociological problems.

5. The subjective meaning of a social relationship may change: for example, a political relationship may turn from one based on solidarity into one based on conflict. But then it is simply a question of terminological convenience and of the de-

65

gree of *continuity* of the change, whether it is said that a new relationship has come into existence or that the old one continues but has acquired new meaning. The meaning, too, can waver between constancy and permanency.

6. The meaningful content which remains relatively constant in a social relationship is capable of being expressed in axioms to which the parties involved can be *expected* to adhere at least approximately by their partners. This is the more likely to be the case, the more rational the conduct is in relation to given values or goals. There is far less possibility of rational formulation of subjective meaning in the case of an erotic attraction or a relation based on personal loyalty or any other emotional type than there is, for example, in the case of a business contract.

7. The meaning of a social relationship can be agreed to by mutual consent. This means that those who participate make promises concerning their future conduct—either toward each other or in any other way. Each participant expects then that normally, and insofar as he behaves rationally, the other participant will orient *his* behavior in accordance with the meaning of the agreement as he—the first participant—understands it. His own behavior is thus partly goal-oriented and he expects to adhere more or less loyally to it; but it is also partly value-related —that is, it is his *duty* to adhere to the agreement in the sense as he understands it. This much may be anticipated; for the rest compare paragraphs 9 and 13 below.

TYPES OF SOCIAL CONDUCT: USAGE, CUSTOM

Within the realm of social conduct one finds certain factual uniformities. That is, there are certain courses of behavior which with a typical identical meaning are repeated by the individuals involved or occur simultaneously among a number of them. It is with such types of conduct that sociology is concerned, in contrast to history which is interested in the causal connections of important, i.e., fateful, single events.

An actually existing probability of the uniformity of an orientation of social conduct will be called "usage," where, and insofar as the probability arises, its existence within a group of people is based on nothing but actual habit. Usage will be called "custom" if the actual habit is one of long standing. Where, on the other hand, a usage is determined by the fact that all the parties' conduct is goal-oriented toward identical expectations, it will be called "usage determined by a situation of self-interest on the part of the individual" (*interessenbedingt*).

1. "Fashion" is also a part of usage. Fashion as distinguished from usage exists where the conduct in question is motivated by its novelty rather than by its long standing, as is true with custom. Fashion belongs in the neighborhood of "convention," since it originates for the most part from the desire for social prestige. It need not be further discussed here.

2. In contrast to "convention" and "law" we shall speak of "custom," where the rule is not externally guaranteed but where the individual conforms to it simply unconsciously or for reasons

of simple convenience or whatever the reason may be; but there is always the justified expectation on the part of the members of the groups that a customary rule will be adhered to for the same reasons and in the same way by others. Custom in this sense could not claim real "validity": nobody is "required" to abide by it. Obviously, the transition from this case to those of a valid convention or law is quite gradual. Everywhere what has been traditionally handed down has become the source of what has acquired valid authority. It is customary today that we eat a breakfast of some distinct content every morning; but nobody is "required" to do so, except possibly the guest in a hotel and this too has not always been customary. On the other hand, our manner of dress is today no longer based on mere custom, but has become convention. In this respect, the chapters on usage and custom in the second volume of Ihering's *Zweck im Recht* are still worth reading. See also P. Oertmann, *Rechtsregelung und Verkehrssitte* (1914) and, more recently, E. Weigelin, *Sitte, Recht und Moral* (1919) whose opinions agree with mine and disagree with those of Staemmler.

3. Numerous quite conspicuous uniformities in the course of social behavior are not based at all on the orientation toward some "valid" norm or usage; rather on the fact that the corresponding type of social behavior is, in the nature of the case, best adapted to the normal interests of the individuals involved as they themselves perceive them to be. This is especially true of economic conduct, as for example, of the uniformities of pricing in a "free" market. The distributors thus treat their own conduct as a means for obtaining the satisfaction of ends as defined by what they realize to be their own typical economic interests and similarly treat as conditions the corresponding typical expectations as to the prospective behavior of others. In this way,

the more strictly goal-oriented their conduct, the more will they tend to react similarly to the same situation. Thus there arise similarities, uniformities, and continuities in their attitudes and behavior which are often far more stable than they would be if behavior were oriented to a system of norms and duties which were considered binding on the group. This phenomenon—the fact that orientation in terms of one's own naked self-interest and of that of others causes results which are very similar to those which are attempted through compulsion (often in vain) by an authoritative agency—is of special relevancy in the field of economics. Its observation was, in fact, one of the important origins of economics as a science. But it is similarly true of all areas of behavior. This type of phenomenon in its consciousness and lack of restraint is the direct antithesis of every kind of unthinking commitment to routinized norms, but also of devotion to norms that are consciously accepted as absolute values. An essential component of the rationalization of behavior is the substitution for the unthinking commitment to ancient custom, of planned adaptation to situations in terms of self-interest. Of course, this does not exhaust the concept of the rationalization of behavior. This is so, because in addition such behavior can impinge positively on the conscious realization of ultimate values, or, negatively, not only at the expense of custom, but also of emotional values, and finally, in favor of a value-free type of rationality, at the expense of belief in any absolute values. The many interpretations of the concept of rationalization will continue to be of interest to us. (Further conceptualizations in this context will be found at the end.)

4. The stability of (mere) custom rests essentially on the fact that he who does not adapt his behavior to it is subject to big and little inconveniences and annoyances as long as the behavior

of a majority of those surrounding him continue to adhere to this custom and conform to it.

Similarly, the stability of any conduct in terms of self-interest rests on the fact that the person who does not "take into consideration" the interests of others arouses their hostility, or that he may end up in a situation different from that which he had contemplated and therefore runs the risk of damaging his own interests.

⟦ Paragraph 5

THE CONCEPT OF LEGITIMATE AUTHORITY

Conduct, especially social conduct, and more particularly a social relationship, can be oriented on the part of the individuals to what constitutes their "idea" of the existence of a *legitimate authority*. The probability that such orientation actually occurs shall be called the "validity" of the authority in question.

1. That an authority assumes "validity" must therefore mean more than the mere regularity of social conduct as determined by custom or self-interest. The fact that furniture movers advertise their services regularly about the time that leases expire is caused quite clearly by their desire to exploit an opportunity in their self-interest. The fact that a peddler regularly visits a certain customer on a certain day of the week or month is either the result of long habit or of self-interest (e.g. the turnover in his district). When a civil servant shows up at his office every day at the same time, it may be determined not only by custom or self-interest, since he can hold to that as he pleases, but it may be partly the result of his abiding by the office regulations which impose certain duties on him and which he may be loath to violate, since such conduct would not only be disadvantageous to him but may be also abhorrent to his "sense of duty," which, to a greater or lesser extent, represents for him an absolute value.

2. Only then will the content of a social relationship represent "authority," if its conduct can be oriented approximately toward certain recognizable axioms. Only then will such author-

ity acquire "validity," if the orientation toward these axioms includes at least the recognition that they are binding on the individual or the corresponding behavior constitutes a model worthy of imitation. Indeed, conduct may be oriented toward an authority for a variety of motives. But the fact that along with other motives the authority is also held by at least some of the other individuals as being worthy of imitation or binding naturally increases to a very considerable degree the probability that conduct will in fact conform to it. An authority which is obeyed for the sole reason of expedience is generally much less stable than one which is upheld on a purely customary basis. The latter attitude toward authority is much the most common one. But even more stable is the type of conduct oriented toward custom, which enjoys the prestige of being considered exemplary or binding, or possesses what is known as "legitimacy." Of course, the transition from a goal- or tradition-oriented conduct to one motivated by a belief in its legitimacy is extremely gradual.

3. There can be orientation toward valid authority even where its meaning (as generally understood) is not necessarily obeyed. The probability that the authority is to some extent held as a valid norm can also have its effect on behavior even where its meaning is evaded or deliberately violated. This may be true at first even on the basis of sheer expediency. Thus the thief's behavior exemplifies the validity of the criminal law merely by the fact that he tries to conceal his conduct. The very fact that an authority is valid within a particular group makes it necessary for him to practice concealment. This is, of course, a marginal case and frequently the authority is violated partially only in one or another respect or its violation is sought to be passed off as legitimate with a varying measure of good faith. Or there may really coexist various interpretations of the mean-

ing of authority alongside of each other. In that case the sociologist will regard each one as valid exactly insofar as it actually shapes the course of behavior. It is no great difficulty for the sociologist to recognize within the same social group the existence of several, possibly mutually contradictory, valid systems of authority. Indeed it is possible even for the same individual to orient his behavior to mutually contradictory systems of authority. This can take place not only in short succession, as can be observed daily, but even in the case of the same conduct. A person who engages in a duel orients his behavior toward the observance of the honor code; but he also orients his conduct toward the criminal law by keeping the duel a secret or, conversely, by voluntarily appearing in court. Where, however, evasion or violation of the system of authority in its generally understood meaning has become the rule, such authority can be said to be "valid" only in a limited sense or has ceased to be valid altogether. For the jurist a system of authority is either valid or it is not; for the sociologist no such choice exists. Rather, there is a gradual transition between the two extremes of validity and non-validity and it is possible for mutually contradictory systems of authority to coexist validly. Each one is valid precisely in proportion to the probability that behavior will be actually oriented toward it.

Those familiar with the literature will remember the role played by the concept of authority in R. Staemmler's work, which, brilliant as it may be, is nevertheless misleading and confuses the problems in a disastrous manner. (See above, my prefatory remarks.)

Staemmler does not only fail to distinguish between the normative meaning of validity and the empirical one, but he also misunderstands that social conduct is oriented to other things besides systems of authority. Above all, he treats authority, quite

73

illogically, as a form of social conduct and then tries to relate it typically to "content" in a way that is analogous to that of form and content in the theory of knowledge, not to mention other errors. Indeed, conduct which is, primarily economic, for example, is oriented to the concept of the relative scarcity of certain available means for the satisfaction of wants in proportion to the contemplated conduct of the individual and to the present and probable behavior of others, insofar as the latter affect the same resources. Of course, such conduct is, in addition, oriented in its choice of economic procedures to the conventional and legal rules recognized as valid or whose violation, it is known, would call forth certain reactions by other persons.

This extremely simple empirical subject matter Staemmler has succeeded in confusing hopelessly, especially due to his assertion that a causal relationship between authority and empirical social conduct is a conceptual impossibility. It is true, of course, that between the legally-orthodox normative validity of a system of authority and any empirical process there is really no causal relationship to be found. In that context there exists only the question of whether the system of authority as correctly interpreted in the legal sense "applies" also to the empirical situation. The question is whether it should be treated as "valid" in a normative sense and, if so, what the content of its normative prescriptions ought to be. However, between the probability that social behavior is oriented toward the subjective belief in the validity of authority and social behavior which is economically oriented there is of course a causal relationship. But for sociological purposes it is exactly such a probability of orientation toward the subjective belief in the validity of an authority which constitutes the valid authority itself.

TYPES OF LEGITIMATE AUTHORITY:
CONVENTION, LAW

The legitimacy of authority can be guaranteed in the following
ways:

I. On a purely subjective basis, i.e., it may be due to: 1)
merely affectual, or emotional surrender, or 2) it may derive
from a rational belief in the absolute validity of the authority
as an expression of ultimate, binding values of an ethical, aesthetic or of any other kind; or 3) it may originate in religious
attitudes, i.e., guided by the belief that salvation depends on
obedience to authority.

II. Also, the legitimacy of authority may be guaranteed by
self-interest, i.e., in the expectation of specific consequences of
a particular kind.

A system of authority will apear to be *a*) *conventional*, where
its validity is externally guaranteed by the probability that deviation from it within a definable social group will be met with
relatively general and significantly perceptible disapproval. *b*)
Such a system of authority will be considered as *law* if it is externally guaranteed by the probability that unusual behavior
will be met by physical or psychic sanctions aimed at compelling
conformity or at punishing disobedience and administered by a
group of men especially charged with the authority for that purpose. (On the concept of convention see Ihering, op. cit.,
Weigelin, op. cit., and also F. Toennies, *Die Sitte*, 1909.)

1. The term "convention" will be used to designate that part

of custom which, within a given social group, is approved as valid and guaranteed against violation by sanctions of disapproval. It differs from *law*, as defined here, by the absence of a group whose specialized function is that of enforcement. Staemmler's distinction of convention from law according to whether or not submission is voluntary, corresponds neither to common linguistic usage nor does it accord with his own illustration. Conformity with convention in such matters as the usual forms of salutation, decent fashions, and various rules governing social intercourse, in form as well as in content, is expected to be taken seriously by the individual and regarded as binding by him. Unlike the choice in the manner of cooking, this is not a case where he is free to either accept or reject common usage. A violation of convention, for example of professional ethics, often meets with the most effective and serious retribution in the form of social ostracism, which may be even more effective than legal sanction. What is lacking is merely the group whose specialized function is that of upholding law and order, such as judges, prosecutors, administrative officials, and executioners. However, there is no clear dividing line to be found here. The marginal case of a *conventional* guarantee of an authority in the process of transition to a *legal* guarantee of authority is to be found in the application of the formally threatened and organized boycott. But in our terminology this already constitutes a means of legal coercion. It is irrelevant in the present context that in certain instances a convention may, in addition to mere disapproval, also be protected by other means, as for example in the case of the master of the house who expels the visitor whose conduct appears to him as unconventional. What is decisive in this case is that a single individual, by virtue of conventional disapproval applies these—often very drastic sanctions—not as a member of an organized group endowed with specific authority, but merely on the basis of his own authority.

2. In our context, the concept of law will be defined in terms of the existence of a special enforcement agency. In other contexts different definitions may well be appropriate. The character of this enforcement agency need not, of course, be similar to what we are familiar with today. In particular, it is unnecessary that there should be any judicial organ. Thus in the case of a blood feud, the clan becomes such an enforcement agency, provided that its behavior in such situations is actually governed by some set of rules. But this is an extreme case that can only just barely be considered "legal coercion." It is well known that international law has always been denied the quality of law precisely because it lacks a superior supra-national enforcement agency. Indeed, in terms of our definition this would certainly be true of a system of authority whose legitimacy is based entirely on the expectation of disapproval and reprisals on the part of those who are injured by its violation, i.e., where conduct is guaranteed entirely by convention and expediency rather than a specialized enforcement agency. But for purposes of legal terminology the opposite usage might well be acceptable.

In any case, the means of enforcement are quite irrelevant. Even the "friendly persuasion" that can be found in various religious sects as a form of gentle pressure on sinners constitutes coercion in our sense, provided it is carried out according to the rules and by a specially designated group. The same is true of the use of censure as a means of enforcing norms of moral conduct, and even more so of psychic pressure brought to bear as a means of church discipline. Hence, law may be guaranteed by ecclesiastical as well as by political authority and it may be guaranteed by the statutes of an association or through the authority of the head of the household. The rules of a fraternal organization are as much law in our sense as are those duties that are legally regulated but non-enforceable and which are mentioned in Article 888, sec. 2 of the German Code of Civil Procedure. The *leges imperfectae* and the category of natural obligations are forms of legal terminology which indirectly express limits or conditions on the use of compulsion. A forcibly introduced "traffic law" is nevertheless law. (See Par. 157, 242, Civil Code [*Buergerliches Gesetzbuch*] on the concept of common law obligations, i.e., obligations which arise out of community standards of acceptable behavior and in this way obtain legal sanction. See also the article by Max Rumelin in *Schwaebische Heimatsgabe fuer Theodor Haering*, 1918.)

3. Not every valid authority is necessarily of an abstract general character. The distinction between a legal precept and a specific judicial decision has not been made always and everywhere as clearly as we have come to expect today. Authority may thus arise simply on the basis of the authority governing a single concrete situation. The details of this subject are the concern of the sociology of law. But for our purposes the modern distinction between a legal precept and a specific decision will be taken for granted unless otherwise indicated.

4. A system of authority which is guaranteed by external sanctions may also become internalized. The relationship between law, convention and ethics does not present any problems to the sociologist. The sociologist regards a standard as "ethical" if men attribute to it a specific kind of value which they claim to be ethically good, just as any conduct regarded as beautiful can be measured by aesthetic standards. Ethically normative ideas of this kind can have a powerful influence on conduct, even though they may lack any external guarantees. This is frequently the

case when the violation of such standards does not seriously affect the interests of others.

On the other hand, such ethical standards are also often sanctioned by religious beliefs. But they may also be upheld by such conventional means as disapproval of the violation followed by boycott, or by legal means such as police action and the sanctions applied by civil and criminal law. Every really sociologically valid ethical system is likely to rest on convention, that is, on the probability of widespread disapproval following its violation. Not every conventionally or legally sanctioned norm claims, however, to be one of ethics. Legal norms are frequently motivated by mere expediency and can thus lay even less claim to an ethical character than do conventional norms. Whether or not a socially accepted normative authority belongs in the realm of ethics or is mere convention or law, can only be decided empirically in terms of what is actually held to be "ethical" by the group under investigation. But it is not possible to state any generalization in this respect.

THE VALIDITY OF LEGITIMATE AUTHORITY:
TRADITION, FAITH, LAW

A system of authority can legitimately assume validity in the eyes of those subject to it in a variety of ways:

a) by tradition: that which has always existed is valid.

b) by virtue of emotional attachment, legitimizing the validity of what has been newly proclaimed or is considered worthy of imitation.

c) by virtue of a rational belief in its absolute value: what has been revealed as being absolutely valid *is* valid.

d) because of a form of positive proclamation whose legality is recognized as being beyond questioning. Such legality can be regarded as legitimate either 1) because it has been agreed to voluntarily by all those concerned, or 2) because it has been imposed on the basis of what is held to be a legitimate authority by some people over others and therefore exercises a corresponding claim to their obedience.

All other details except for a few other concepts that need definition, will be discussed below in the sociology of law and the sociology of power. At present the following brief remarks will suffice.

1. The oldest and most universally held legitimacy of authority is based on the sacredness of tradition. Fear of magical penalties strengthens the psychological inhibitions regarding changes in customary modes of behavior. At the same time a system of

authority continues as valid because of the many vested interests which arise with respect to its perpetuation.

2. Conscious creations of new authorities were originally almost entirely the result of prophetic oracles or at least of revelations enjoying the nimbus of prophecy, as was true as late as the statutes of the Hellenic Aisymnetes. Compliance then depended upon the faith in the legitimacy of the prophet. In periods of strict traditionalism no new system of authority could thus arise without new revelations being proclaimed in this way, unless the new system of authority was not really looked upon as new but was regarded instead as a truth that had already been valid but temporarily obscured and which was now being restored to its rightful place.

3. The archetype of absolutely value-related legitimacy is found in the idea of "natural law." The influence of its logically developed positions upon actual behavior may not always be in accord with its ideal claims, but it cannot be denied that its influence has been far from negligible; these ideal claims therefore must be clearly distinguished from those of revealed, enacted, or traditional law.

4. Today, the most common form of legitimacy is the *belief* in *legality*, i.e., the compliance with enactments which are formally correct and which have been imposed by an accustomed procedure. The contrast between voluntarily agreed upon rules and those which are imposed from without is strictly relative. In the past, for an authority to be treated as legitimate it was often necessary for it to have been accepted unanimously. Today, however, it frequently happens that an authority is accepted by a majority of the members of a group with the minority, which holds different opinions, merely acquiescing. In such cases the authority is actually imposed by the majority on the

minority. Very frequent also is the case of a violent, ruthless or simply energetic minority imposing an authority which eventually comes to be regarded as legitimate by those who originally opposed it. Where voting is the legal method of creating or changing a system of authority, it happens frequently that the will of the minority achieves a formal majority to which the real majority acquiesces: in this case "majority rule" becomes mere sham. The belief in a contractual system of authority can be traced to fairly ancient times and can also be found among so-called primitive peoples, but in such cases it is almost always supplemented by the authority of oracles.

5. Compliance with authority imposed by any one man or several, insofar as it does not depend on mere fear or is derived from motives of expediency, always presupposes a belief in the legitimate authority of the source imposing it.

6. As a rule, compliance with authority is almost invariably determined by a combination of motives, such as a self-interest, or a mixture composed of adherence to tradition and a belief in legality, unless it is a case of entirely new principles. Very often those who comply thus with authority are not even aware of whether they do so because of custom, convention, or law. It then becomes the task of the sociologist to analyze that basis of validity which is most typical.

THE CONCEPT OF STRUGGLE

A social relationship will be called a *struggle* insofar as the behavior of one party is oriented purposefully toward making his
own will prevail against the resistance of other parties or another
party. If the means of such struggle do not consist in actual
physical violence then the process is one of "peaceful" struggle.
This "peaceful" struggle will be called "competition" if it is
carried on as a formally peaceful attempt to obtain control over
opportunities and advantages which are also coveted by others.
A competition will be known as "controlled competition" if
its means and ends are subject to the same authority. This
frequently latent social or individual struggle for advantages
and for survival, without being necessarily based on a conflict
of interest, will be called "selection"; insofar as it is a question
of the relative opportunities of individuals during their own
lifetime, it is a form of "social selection"; insofar as it concerns
the varying probability of the survival of inherited characteristics, it is a form of "biological selection."

1. A great variety of transitional stages exist, ranging from
bloody combat unrestrained by any rules and aiming at the complete annihilation of the enemy to the conventionally regulated
tournament of the Middle Ages (viz. the classic call of the her-
ald before the battle of Fontenay: "Messieurs les Anglais, tirez
les premiers!"), as well as to the strict rules of the game governing a sport. Other examples of such transitions are the unrestrained erotic competition of suitors for the favor of a woman,

the economic competition bound by the rules of the market place, or the strictly regulated competitions for artistic awards, and finally the hard won victory of the election campaign. The conceptual differentiation of violent, physical struggle is justified by the uniqueness of its normally used means and the corresponding peculiarities of the sociological consequences of its use.

2. All forms of struggle and all manner of competition which occur typically on a large scale will lead, eventually, regardless of the decisive importance of chance in individual cases, to a singling out of all those who possess to a higher degree those personal qualities important to success. The nature of these qualities is determined by the conditions of the struggle or competition which include, besides any and all imaginable individual or mass qualities, also those of the systems of authority toward which the behavior of individuals is oriented either by virtue of tradition, faith or expediency. Thus, qualities necessary may be those of physical strength, unscrupulousness, the level of mental ability, sheer lung power or demagogic technique, greater loyalty to superiors than to the fickle masses, more creative originality rather than social adaptability; in short, those qualities are necessary which are either unusual or are typical of mediocrity. Any type of authority influences differently the opportunities for social selection.

Not *every* social selection process is a "struggle" in our sense of the word. For the present, "social selection" means only: that certain types of behavior and, eventually, of personal qualities are favored in their ability to procure certain advantages in attaining a social relationship; for example in the role of lover, husband, deputy, civil servant, general manager, successful businessman, etc. Whether or not this social advantage was achieved through "struggle" is not discernible from the process of social selection; nor is it possible to determine whether it affects the biological chances for survival in one way or another.

It is only where genuine competition exists that the term "struggle" applies. Only in the sense of selection does it appear that, on the basis of all experience, struggle is inevitable and only in the sense of biological selection that it is inevitable in principle. Selection is perpetual precisely because no means seems to exist that can remove it completely. Even for a strictly pacifist system of authority it is possible to regulate the means, directions and objectives of struggle only by dealing with each type separately. This means that there are other ways of struggling toward victory provided the process of competition remains open. But even if it were assumed, utopistically, that competition could be completely eliminated, such conditions as prevail would still lead to a latent process of selection, either biological or social, and which would favor the types best adapted to these conditions, regardless of environmental or hereditary qualities. Social selection, empirically, and biological selection, in principle, act as obstacles to the complete elimination of struggle.

3. Struggle and the selection process occurring in social relationships are to be distinguished naturally from the struggle of the individual for survival and success. Only in a metaphorical sense can these concepts be applied to social relationships. For relationships exist only as systems of human behavior with particular subjective meanings. Therefore a process of selection or struggle between them signifies that a specific type of conduct is being displaced by another, whether it is conduct by the same or other persons. This is done in a variety of ways. Human conduct may be aimed first, at the conscious alteration of certain social relationships or at the prevention of their crea-

tion or perpetuation; for example, a "state" may be destroyed through war or revolution, a conspiracy through bloody suppression; concubinage through police measure; usurous business practices through denial of legal protection and through the imposition of penalties; again, social relationships may be influenced by the deliberately favored treatment of one social group over another. Such goals can be pursued either by individuals or by organized groups. Secondly, it may be the unintentional by-product of a course of human conduct and the conditions giving rise to it that provide certain concrete social relationships with a decreasing chance to continue or with the chance of being created anew. All changes of natural and social conditions have some sort of effect on the chances for survival of social relationships. Anyone is free to regard such instances as a process of "selection." An example would be to say that among several states the "strongest," in the sense of being the most "adaptable," will emerge victorious. But it should be remembered that this so-called selection has nothing to do with the selection of human types in either the social or biological sense; in every case it will remain necessary to inquire into the causes which have led up to a change in the chances of survival of one or another form of social behavior or relationship, what causes are responsible for the breaking up of a social relationship, or have permitted it to continue at the expense of other competing forms. The explanation of such causal processes involves so many facets that it would seem wise not to encompass them with one single term; otherwise, one runs the danger of introducing uncritical value-judgments into empirical investigations and risks generalizations from a particular case that happens to rest on merely "accidental" circumstances. That type of argument has, unfortunately, become increasingly frequent in recent years. The fact that a given social relationship has been eliminated for reasons that are characteristic only of a particular situation tells us, after all, nothing about the "survival" value of such a relationship.

❨ Paragraph 9

COMMUNALIZATION AND AGGREGATION
OF SOCIAL RELATIONSHIPS

The *communalization* of social relationships occurs if and insofar as the orientation of social behavior—whether in the individual case, on the average or in the ideal type—is based on a
sense of solidarity: the result of emotional or traditional attach-
ments of the participants. The *aggregation* of social relationships
on the other hand, is the result of a reconciliation and a balanc-
ing of interests which are motivated either by rational value-
judgments or expediency. Typically, aggregation may, but need
not, rest on rational agreement arrived at by mutual consent. In
that case "aggregated" conduct will be either value-oriented,
i.e., based on faith in the binding validity of the obligation to
adhere to it, or it will be goal-oriented on the expectation that
the other party will live up to it.

1. This terminology is reminiscent of the differentiation
made by F. Toennies in his pioneering work *Gemeinschaft und
Gesellschaft*. However, for the purposes of his investigation he
has given this distinction a rather more specific meaning than
would be convenient for the purposes of the present discussion.

The purest types of aggregative relationships can be found
in the *a*) strictly expedient nature of the free market exchange:
this is usually a compromise of opposed but complementary
interests; or in *b*) the purely voluntary union based on self-
interest, whose goal is the promotion of the specific material interests (e.g., economic) of its members; and in *c*) the volun-

tary union based on absolute ideological values—for example, a rationally oriented sect which ignores emotional or affectual interests but devotes itself only to a "cause"; only in exceptional cases does the last occur in anything approaching an ideal type.

2. *Communalization* may be based on any kind of emotional, affectual or traditional link: e.g. a spiritual brotherhood, an erotic relationship, a relation of personal loyalty, a national heritage, or the comradeship of a military unit. This type is found most conveniently in the family relation. Of course, the great majority of social relationships shares both communal and aggregative factors. No matter how expedient and sober the ruling considerations in such a relationship may be—e.g., that of customer to clerk—it will be open to the introduction of emotional values which reach beyond mere arbitrary utility. Every social relationship which goes beyond the pursuit of immediately obtainable common ends involves a relative degree of permanency between the same persons and such relations cannot be limited to activities of a purely technical nature. Such a tendency can be observed in the case of aggregation within the same military unit or in the same school class, or the same office and shop, though the intensity (of communalization) varies considerably. Conversely, it is possible for a social relationship of primarily communal character, to manifest a type of behavior on the part of its members which is, either wholly or in part, motivated by considerations of expediency. For example, great differences can be found in the extent to which the members of a family group feel a genuine community of interests or, instead, exploit their status as a "social unit" for purely personal ends. The concept of communalization is here held deliberately vague and consequently includes a very heterogeneous group of phenomena.

3. Communalization is, in the sense used here, normally the direct opposite of "struggle." This should not be allowed, however, to mislead us into thinking that actual coercion cannot normally be found even in the closest of such communal relationships if one party is more yielding than the other; also that the process of selection of types, leading to differences in opportunity and survival, does not continue within these relationships just as it does anywhere else. Aggregation, on the other hand, represents merely the reconciliation of competing interests, in which case only a part of the object or the means of the struggle is eliminated, (or at least the attempt is made toward such elimination), but the real conflict of interests with its attendant competition for opportunities remains unchanged. Struggle and community are relative concepts; a struggle may take various forms, depending on the means used, either peaceful or violent, and the degree of ruthlessness with which they are employed. As stated previously, any type of authority governing social behavior leaves room for the ideal process of selection in the competition between various rival human types.

4. It is by no means true that the sharing of common qualities, a common situation or of common modes of behavior imply the existence of a communal social relationship. For example, the possession of common inherited biological characteristics which are suitable for the establishment of racial distinctions for certain persons do not imply in any way a communal social relationship between them. By restrictions on their right to trade or intermarry such persons may find themselves in the same situation, that is, one of isolation from their familiar environment which imposes such restrictions. But even if they all react to this situation in the same way, this does not constitute a communal relationship created by the merely common "feeling" about the

situation and its consequences. It is only when this feeling leads to mutual orientation of their behavior toward each other that communal relationship arises among them. This is especially true of the Jews who, except for some Zionists and the activities of some specifically Jewish interest organizations, experience only a relatively small sense of communal relationship; as a matter of fact, Jews often repudiate the existence of a Jewish community.

Community of language as a result of a similarity of tradition through family and surrounding social environment, facilitates mutual understanding and promotes therefore to the highest degree, all types of social relationships. By itself language is not sufficient to bring about communalization, but merely eases the communication between the groups concerned and, therefore, the creation of more aggregation. It does this through the contact of individuals, not because they speak the same language but because they share other kinds of interests. Orientation to the rules of a common language is primarily useful as a means of communication, but not sufficient to provide the substance of social relationships. It is only the emergence of conscious differences vis-à-vis other persons, that the fact of two individuals speaking a different language and in this respect sharing a common situation can lead them to experience a feeling of community and create modes of social organization that are consciously based on the sharing of a common language.

The participation in a market is again of a different type. It encourages aggregations of different individuals to engage in specific acts of exchange and in a social relationship, especially that of competition, between the prospective buyers, whose behavior must be mutually oriented to each other. Beyond that we can speak of aggregation only to the extent that some individual participants enter into agreements in order to pursue their advantage in a price war, or to secure and regulate all transactions under conditions favorable to them alone. As a matter of fact, the free market and the competitive economy based on it, form the most important type of reciprocal influence of behavior in terms of pure self-interest so typical of modern economies.

OPEN AND CLOSED SOCIAL RELATIONSHIPS

A social relationship, regardless of whether it is communal or aggregative, will be known as "open" to those on the outside, if, and insofar as, participation in the mutually oriented social conduct, relevant to its subjective meaning, is, according to its system of authority, not denied to anyone who is inclined to participate and is actually in a position to do so. The relationship will be known as "closed," on the other hand, to those on the outside, so far as and to the extent that within the range of its subjective meaning and the validity of its authority, the participation of certain persons is excluded, limited, or subject to conditions. The open or closed character of a social relationship may depend on tradition or affectual attitudes, or it may be value-related or based on pure expediency. It is most likely to be closed for rational reasons in the following situations: a social relationship may provide those participating with the opportunity of satisfying many diverse interests, whether the satisfactions be spiritual or material, the participation either for reasons of expediency or because of some ulterior consequences, or whether it is achieved through cooperation or by reconciliation of interests. If the participants, through the admission of outsiders expect that it will lead to an improvement of their situation either in the degree, the kind, the security or the value of the satisfaction, they will be interested in keeping the relationship open. If, conversely, they are interested in improving their position through monopolistic practices they will tend to favor a *closed* relationship.

A closed social relationship is capable of guaranteeing its monopolized advantages to its members through *a*) competition freely engaged in within the group; *b*) regulation or rationing of such advantages; and *c*) their appropriation by individuals or small groups on a permanent basis, in which case they become more or less inalienable. This last case is a closure within, as well as against outsiders. Such appropriated advantages will be called "rights." In keeping with the prevailing system of authority, appropriation of these rights may be extended for the benefit of specific communal or aggregative groups (e.g., household groups) or for the benefit of individuals. In the latter case, such rights are enjoyed by the individual on a purely personal basis, or in such a way that in case of his death one or more other persons related to the holder of the right by birth (kinship), or by some other social relationship, may inherit the rights in question. Or these rights may pass to one or more individuals specifically designated by the original holder. Finally, it may be that the original holder is more or less fully empowered to alienate his rights voluntarily, either to other individuals or to anyone he chooses. This is known as alienable appropriation.

The active participant in a closed social relationship will be called a member; but if the participation is regulated in such a way as to guarantee him appropriated advantages, he will be called a lawful member with rights and privileges. Appropriated advantages, which are enjoyed by individuals through inheritance or by hereditary groups, will be called the "property" of the individual or of the group in question; insofar as they are "alienable," they are "free" property.

The apparently "laborious" definition of these concepts is an example that what is "self-evident" is rarely thought out clearly, for the very reason that it appears obvious.

98

1. *a*) Communal relationships which tend toward closeness by virtue of tradition are, for example, those in which membership is determined by family ties.

   b) Personal relationships of an emotional nature, e.g., those based on love or loyalty, are usually effectually closed.

   c) Value-related closure is usually characteristic of a group sharing a common religious belief system.

   d) Goal-oriented closure is typical of economic associations of a monopolistic or plutocratic character.

Here are a few examples chosen at random. The open or closed character of verbal communications depends on their content; thus, general conversation is apt to be open while a more intimate conversational exchange or business communication tends to be closed. Market relationships are usually, at least at first, of an open nature. In numerous cases of both communal and aggregative relationships we can observe a phase of exclusiveness alternating with one of expansion; for example, in the case of the guilds and the democratic city-states of antiquity and of the middle ages, there was a tendency at times to increase their membership in the interest of improving the security of their position of power, at other times to restrict their membership to protect the value of their monopolistic position. The same phenomenon is not uncommon in monastic orders and religious sects which have changed from a stage of religious proselytizing to one of exclusiveness, either in the interest of maintaining a high ethical standard or for the protection of material benefits. The expansion of the market relationship for purposes of a larger turnover or its contraction for monopolistic practices is a similar case in point. The promotion of linguistic uniformity is today a natural result of publishing and writing interests and can be contrasted with the earlier, not uncommon, tendency for certain classes to maintain linguistic peculiarities or even resort to secret languages.

2. Both the extent and the method of regulation and the exclusion of outsiders may vary widely, so that the transition from an open to a regulated or closed condition is gradual. Various requirements for admission may be laid down: qualifying tests, probationary periods, the purchase of a share subject to certain conditions, election of new members by ballot, eligibility based on ancestry or by virtue of achievement, and in the case of internally directed restrictiveness contingent on the appropriation of rights within the group, status may depend on acquisition of such an appropriated right. Any number of varieties of closure or of conditions for admission can be found. Thus regulation and closure are relative concepts. There are all kinds of transitional stages ranging from the exclusive club or the theater audience, whose members have bought tickets, to the rally of a campaigning party, which is open to the largest possible number of people; similarly, from a church service open to the public through the rituals of a limited sect and to the mysteries of a secret cult.

3. Restrictiveness within the group—as between members themselves and in their relations to each other—may also assume the most diverse forms. For example, a caste, guild, or an association of stockbrokers which is closed to outsiders, may permit its members to compete freely for all the advantages which the group as a whole monopolizes for itself; or it may restrict every member for life or on a hereditary basis only to the enjoyment of certain advantages, such as access to customers or to particular business opportunities. This is especially characteristic of India. Similarly, a closed group of settlers may allow its members free

use of the soil, or it may restrict them rigidly to a specific share of the acreage per family. Here, too, all conceivable transitional and intermediate forms can be found. Historically, for example, the restriction within the group of prospective claimants to a fief, a living and offices, and the appropriation on the part of those enjoying them, have occurred in the most varied forms. In the same way, the establishment of rights to and possession of particular jobs on the part of the worker develop all the way from the closed shop to a right to a particular job. The emergence of the work councils may be, though it need not be, a first step in this direction. A preparatory stage could be the prohibition to dismiss a worker without the consent of the workers' representatives.

Details here belong to the objective analysis of individual cases. The most extreme form of permanent appropriation exists where particular rights are guaranteed to the individual or to certain groups of them, such as household, clan, or family, in such a way that by law, in the case of death, the rights descend to specific heirs or the possessor is free to transfer them to any other person at will; the latter *thereby* becomes a party to the social relationship, so that when appropriation has reached the extreme *within* the group, it becomes a relatively *open* group in relation to outsiders. This is true as long as the acquisition of membership is not bound to the consent of other members.

4. The principal motivations for a restrictive social relationship are: *a*) the maintenance of quality and eventually that of prestige and the opportunity deriving from it to enjoy honor and possibly even profit. Examples of this kind are: communities of ascetics, monastic orders, especially, for example, the Indian mendicant orders, religious sects like the Puritans, organized groups of veterans, of ministers, and of other bureaucrats, organ-

ized bodies of citizens as in the Greek city-states, and artisan guilds; *b*) the scarcity of opportunities in relation to the needs of consumption; examples here are monopolies of consumption, the archetype being that of the self-subsistent village community; and *c*) the scarcity of opportunities for gaining a livelihood, and classic examples of this are the monopolization of trade by the guilds, such as the ancient practice of monopolizing fishing rights, etc. Usually motive (*a*) is found in conjunction with (*b*) or (*c*).

⟪ Paragraph 11

ACCOUNTABILITY FOR SOCIAL CONDUCT:
REPRESENTATION

A social relationship, depending on whether it is governed by
traditional or legal authority, may result in certain types of behavior by some of those involved in the relationship, which in
turn will have consequences that affect the conduct of others.
It may be that all are held responsible for the conduct of any
one of them, in which case the condition will be known as "collective solidarity"; or, the conduct of certain individual members, the "representatives," may be binding on the others, i.e.,
those who are being "represented." In such a case, the representatives will be held responsible for both failure and success
of their conduct.

Plenary power may be conferred in accordance with prevailing
authority in such a way that *a*) it becomes appropriated in all its
forms—this is true of autonomous authority, or, *b*) it may be
conferred in accordance with specific standards, permanently
or for a limited term—this is the case with "delegated authority"; or *c*) it may be conferred by specific acts of the members
or of other persons, again either permanently or for a limited
term, as in the case of an appointment.

Concerning the condition under which social relationships
—either communal or aggregative—develop ties of solidarity
or representation, the following can be stated with some degree
of certainty: One of the most decisive conditions is undoubtedly
the extent to which the behavior of the group is directed toward

violent conflict or peaceful exchange as its goal. In addition, there are many special circumstances that may be of crucial importance but which can be discussed only in great detail. Naturally, such a development is least conspicuous in groups which pursue their goals by purely peaceful means. The phenomenon of solidarity and representation often corresponds to that of closure toward outsiders; but this is by no means always the case.

1. The "attribution" of responsibility may, in practice, involve both active and passive solidarity: all the participants may be held responsible for the conduct of any one of them, just as he himself is, and similarly they may be entitled to enjoy any benefits resulting from his conduct. Such responsibility may be owed to the spirits or to the gods, in which case it is of a religious orientation. Or, it may be responsibility owed to human beings based on *convention*, as is true, for example, of a vendetta carried out against or with the help of members of the kinship group, or of reprisals against the inhabitants of a town or the country of an offender; again, it may be responsibility owed to human beings based on *law*, as is illustrated by the formal punishment of relatives, members of the households, or fellow members of the communal group, instead of or in addition to the actual offender, and personal liability of members of a household or of a business partnership for each other's debts. Solidarity vis-à-vis the gods has also had very significant historical results. Thus, for example, in the covenant of Israel with Jahveh, in early Christianity, and in the early Puritan community.

On the other hand, the attribution of solidarity may mean at the very least that the participants in a closed social relationship, either because of traditional or legal authority, are held legally entitled to enjoy some kind of access to advantages and benefits, especially economic ones, which a representative has procured;

examples are the validity of the power exercised by the board of directors of a corporation, or by the responsible agent of a political or economic association over resources which, as authorized, are intended to serve the corporate purpose of the group.

2. The fact of solidarity is found typically in *a*) traditional, communal groups based on heredity or the sharing of a common life: e.g., the household or clan; *b*) closed relationships which monopolize opportunities and ensuing benefits by their own power—this is typical of corporate political groups, especially in the past, though today they exist most strikingly during war time; *c*) in profit-making organizations whose members still personally conduct the business, i.e., a business partnership; and *d*) under certain circumstances, in labor organizations, e.g., an artel. The fact of representation exists most typically in associations devoted to specific purposes and in legally organized groups, especially when funds for a purpose have been collected and must be administered in the interests of the group. More about this in the sociology of law.

3. Plenary power is delegated according to special standards when it goes by seniority or some such similar criteria.

4. The details of this subject matter are not to be treated generally but must be analyzed individually by the sociologist. The most ancient and most universal phenomenon in this field is that of reprisal, either in the form of revenge or as a means of gaining hostages to prevent further injury.

THE CONCEPT OF THE CORPORATE GROUP
AND ITS TYPES

The term "corporate group" will be reserved for a social relationship which is either closed to outsiders or restricts their admission by regulations, and whose authority is enforced by the actions of specific individuals charged with this function, for example, a chief or head and usually also an administrative staff. These functionaries normally will also exercise plenary powers. The incumbency of an executive position or the participation in the functions of the administrative staff constitute "governing authority" and can either be appropriated or may be delegated in accordance with the binding rules of the association as laid down in specific criteria or procedures; such delegation may be permanent, for a term, or in order to deal with an emergency situation. "Corporate behavior" is either that of the administrative staff, which by virtue of its governing authority or possession of plenary powers is oriented to executing the terms of its authority, or it is the behavior of the members as directed by the administrative staff.

1. It makes no difference for purposes of conceptualization whether the relationship is of a communal or aggregative character. The presence of a person or persons in positions of recognized authority will be sufficient: such as the head of a family, the board of directors, the managing director, prince, president, or head of a church, whose conduct is concerned with the execution of the laws and regulations governing the corporate group. This criterion is decisive because it is not merely a matter

of *conduct* which is *oriented* toward an authority but which is specifically charged with its *enforcement*. The addition of this element enlarges the concept of a closed social relationship sociologically and is of the greatest importance in practice. For every closed communal or aggregative group is by no means a corporate group: this is not true, for example of an erotic relationship or of a kinship group lacking a formalized system of authority.

2. Whether or not a corporate group "exists" is entirely a matter of the presence of a person in authority, together, possibly, with an administrative staff. More precisely, it exists so far as there is a *probability* that certain designated persons will act in such a way as to express the true meaning of the laws governing the group; in other words, that there are persons who are determined to act in that sense and in no other when the occasion demands it. What causes such orientation, whether it is a case of emotional, traditional or value-related devotion to duty, any one of which may be involved in feudal fealty, loyalty to an office or to service, or whether it is due to expediency, as, for instance, a pecuniary interest in the accompanying salary, is conceptually of no consequence. Terminologically speaking, and within the framework of sociology, the corporate group does not "exist" apart from the probability that a course of behavior oriented in this manner will take place. If there is no probability of this type of behavior on the part of a particular group of persons or of a given individual, there is, terminologically only a social relationship but no corporate group. But as long as there is a probability of such behavior, the corporate group, as a sociological phenomenon, continues to exist, even though there may occur a *complete change in the specific individuals* whose behavior is oriented to the laws and regulations in question. (The manner in which this definition has been attempted has precisely the purpose to include this very phenomenon).

3. *a*) In addition to the behavior of the administrative staff itself or that which takes place under its direction, it is also possible to find other cases where the conduct of the members is intended to guarantee the observance of authority: for instance, contributions or liturgies, i.e., personal services of all kinds, such as jury service or military service.

b) The prevailing valid system of authority may also include norms to which it is expected that the conduct of the members of the corporate group will be oriented in other ways than those pertaining to the affairs of the group as a unit. For example, the state—itself a corporate group—includes regulations governing private enterprise which are not concerned with the enforcement of the state's legal authority as such but with the conduct that serves private interests; this is true of most "civil" law.

In the first case (*a*), it is possible to speak of behavior oriented to corporate affairs; in the second (*b*), of behavior subject to corporate regulations. Only the conduct of the administrative staff itself as well as that deliberately directed by it can be termed "corporate behavior." Examples of such corporate behavior would be participation in any capacity in a war engaged in by a state, or a petition decided on by the executive committee of an association, or a contract entered into by a person in authority and whose validity is considered binding by the members and for whose consequences they are held accountable (see Paragraph 11); furthermore, all adjudication as well as administration belongs in this category. (See also Paragraph 14, below.)

A corporate group may be either autonomous or heteronomous, either autocephalous or heterocephalous. Autonomy means that the authority governing the group has been established by its own members through their own efforts, as opposed to heteronomy, where it has been imposed by an outside agency. Autocephaly signifies that the director and his staff act by the authority of the autonomous order of the corporate group itself and not as in heterocephaly, that they are subject to outside sources of authority. This is true regardless of any other aspects of the relationship.

An example of heterocephaly can be seen in the appointment of the governors of the Canadian provinces by the central government of the Dominion. It is posible for a heterocephalous group to be autonomous and an autocephalous group to be heteronomous. A corporate group can also in both respects occasionally display this characteristic and sometimes the other.

The autocephalous German member states of the Empire were nevertheless heteronomous within the national sphere of authority, but were autonomous within their own sphere in such matters as religion and education. Alsace-Lorraine as long as it was under German jurisdiction—prior to 1918—was autonomous to a limited degree, but it was also hetercephalous to a limited degree, since the governor was appointed by the emperor. All these elements may be present only partially in the same situation. A corporate group, manifesting at one and the same time heteronomous as well as heterocephalous characteristics, as for example, a regiment as part of an army, is best treated as part of the extensive group. Whether or not this is really the case, depends on the actual extent of independence in the orientation of behavior in a particular case and is, terminologically purely a question of convenience.

TYPES OF AUTHORITY IN A CORPORATE G

The statutory rules of an aggregative relationship may originate either through *a*) voluntary agreement or *b*) by imposition from without and subsequent acquiescence. The governing authority of a corporation may claim legitimate power for the imposition of new rules. The so-called "constitution" of a corporate group signifies the existence of the practical probability that such rules as are imposed by the governing authority will be complied with; the degree, kind and conditions giving rise to such probability will vary with the circumstances. Depending on the prevailing system of authority such conditions may specify that certain groups or sections of their members must make themselves heard or express their consent in some way; in addition, there may be any number of other conditions. The statutes of a corporate group can be imposed not only on its members but also on non-members, provided they satisfy certain criteria. Such criteria are most likely to be related to territory and will refer to residence, birth, or the performance of certain actions within that area; in which case, the system of authority will be known to have "territorial validity." A corporate group whose statutes gain validity on the basis of the territorial principle will be known as a "territorial corporate group." This term will be used regardless of how far its claim to authority extends vis-à-vis its own members to matters pertaining *only* to that area. This is at least possible and certainly occurs to some extent.

1. Used within the context of this terminology, *any* authority

ays "imposed" to the extent that it does not originate from voluntary personal agreement of all the individuals concerned. This is true also of the majority decision to which the minority submits. Consequently, there have been long periods when the legitimacy of majority rule has either not been recognized at all or held to be doubtful, as for example, in the estates of the Middle Ages and, until comparatively recently, in the Russian *Obschtschina*.

2. But even formally "free" agreements are frequently the result of imposition, a fact fairly well recognized, as in the case of the *Obschtschina*. Under such circumstances the sociologist is concerned only with the actual state of affairs.

3. The concept of constitution made use of here is also that used by Lassalle. It is not to be confused with the "written" constitution, or, indeed, with constitution in any legal sense. To the sociologist it is merely of importance when and for what purposes, *within what limits*, or possibly under what special conditions (for example, the approval by gods or priests, or the consent of the electorate) the members of the corporate group will submit to the authority of the governor. Furthermore, under what circumstances does the governor have at his disposal the administrative staff, as well as the corporate power, of the group when issuing orders or, more specifically, imposing new rules.

4. The chief examples of the imposition of an authority with purely territorial validity are: the precepts of criminal law and various other legal rulings which require that as criteria for their applicability the person was resident, born, and performed or completed the action within the area controlled by the corporate group.

THE NATURE OF ADMINISTRATIVE AND
REGULATORY AUTHORITY IN CORPORATE GROUPS

A system of authority which regulates corporate behavior will be called an "administrative authority." A system of authority which governs other social behavior, and thereby protects persons who have a stake in the system, shall be called a "regulatory authority." Insofar as a corporate group engages in the former, it will be called an "administrative group," insofar as it is oriented toward the latter, a regulatory group.

1. It is self-evident that the majority of actual corporate groups displays both characteristics. Only the ideal state governed by the rule of law (*Rechtsstaat*), as conceived by the laissez-faire theorists, would be an example of a purely regulatory corporate group. In it, of course, the control of the monetary system would be left entirely to private enterprise.

2. On the concept of corporate behavior see above, Paragraph 12, No. 3. The concept of administrative authority would include all the rules which govern the behavior of the administrative staff, as well as that of the members vis-à-vis the corporate group. This type of member-group relation involves conduct serving only those goals whose achievement is made mandatory by the system of authority governing the group, and for which a positive course of action has been planned in advance with directives for its execution by the administrative staff and by the members. In a completely communist economic system this would embrace all forms of social conduct. On the other hand,

in a laissez-faire state it would include merely the functions of the judges, police, jurors, soldiers, legislators and of the public in the capacity as lawgiver and voters. Generally, administrative and regulatory authority coincides with the distinction that is made in the political corporate group between public and private law.

THE NATURE OF ORGANIZATION:
CORPORATE ORGANIZATION,
VOLUNTARY AND COMPULSORY ASSOCIATION

An "organization" is a system of continuous activity pursuing a goal of a specified kind. A "corporate organization" is an aggregative social relationship characterized by an administrative staff whose activity is oriented exclusively and continuously to achieving the goals of the organization.

A voluntary association (*club*) is a corporate group based on voluntary agreement, whose statutes are valid only for members who have joined it in person. A compulsory association (*institution*) is a corporate group whose statutes can be imposed successfully within a given specified jurisdiction on every individual behavior that conforms to certain distinct criteria.

1. Insofar as the criterion of continuity is made to apply, the administration of political and ecclesiastical affairs as well as of the business of associations is included in the concept of organization.

2. Voluntary and compulsory associations are both corporate groups whose conduct is based on a rational system of authority. Or, more accurately, if a corporate group has a rationally established system of authority, it will be known either as a voluntary or compulsory association. The state is a primary example of a compulsory association (institution) together with all its subordinate heterocephalous groups; this is equally true of the church, provided its system of authority has been rationally

established. The authority governing a compulsory association claims to be valid for anyone who satisfies certain distinct criteria: such as birth, residence, or the use of certain facilities. It is irrelevant whether the individual concerned personally assumed the obligation—as in the case of a voluntary association —nor is it even of importance whether he participated in the creation of the authority. Such authorities are therefore considered to be imposed, in the best meaning of the word. Specifically, a compulsory association can be a corporate group whose limits are defined territorially.

3. The contrast between compulsory and voluntary associations is purely relative. The rules of a voluntary association may affect the interests of non-members and they may indeed be forced to recognize the validity of these rules, either through usurpation, or through the exercise of naked power, or through a process of legal promulgation (e.g., the laws governing market securities).

4. It need hardly be emphasized that the terms voluntary and compulsory association are not meant to cover conceptually every conceivable type of corporate group. They are, as a matter of fact, only polarizations; thus, in the religious sphere the corresponding types are "sect" and "church."

THE CONCEPTS OF POWER AND DOMINATION

By *power* is meant that opportunity existing within a social relationship which permits one to carry out one's own will even against resistance and regardless of the basis on which this opportunity rests.

By *domination* is meant the opportunity to have a command of a given specified content obeyed by a given group of persons. By "discipline" will be meant the opportunity to obtain prompt, and automatic obedience in a predictable form from a given group of persons because of their practiced orientation toward a command.

1. The concept of power is sociologically amorphous. Every conceivable quality of a person and every conceivable combination of circumstances may put someone in a situation where he can demand compliance with his will. The sociological concept of domination consequently must be more precise and can only mean the probability that a *command* will be obeyed.

2. The concept of "discipline" includes the "practiced nature" of uncritical and unresisting *mass* obedience.

The fact of the matter is that domination depends only on the actual presence of one person successfully issuing commands to another; it does not necessarily imply either the existence of an administrative staff or, for that matter, of a corporate group. Usually, however, it is associated with at least one of these. To the extent that the members of a corporate group are subject to the legitimate exercise of such domination it will be called "corporate domination."

1. The head of a household dominates without an administrative staff. A Bedouin chief who receives tribute from caravans, persons, and shipments of goods which pass through his mountain fastness dominates all those changing and indeterminate individuals who, without being associated with each other, happen to have stumbled into a particular situation. He is able to do this by virtue of his loyal retainers, who act, if the occasion demands it, as his administrative staff in enforcing his will. Theoretically, such domination would be conceivable also by one person alone without the help of any administrative staff.

2. If a corporate group possesses an administrative staff, it is always to a certain extent engaged in corporate domination. But the concept is relative. Normally corporate domination is at the same time also an administrative organization. The nature of a corporate group is determined by a variety of factors: the manner in which the administration is carried out, the character of personnel, the objects over which it exercises control, and the extent of effective jurisdiction of its domination. The first two factors in particular are dependent in the highest degree on the way in which authority is legitimized.

TYPES OF POLITICAL AND
RELIGIOUS CORPORATE GROUPS

Corporate domination will be called "political" if, and insofar as, its existence and the validity of its laws within a defined territorial area are guaranteed by an administrative staff through the continuous application and the threat of force. A compulsory political association with a continuous organization will be called a "state" if, and insofar as, its administrative staff successfully claims the monopolization of the legitimate use of physical force in the enforcement of its authority. Social behavior, especially of a corporate group, will be politically oriented, if, and insofar as, its purpose is to influence the leadership of a corporate political group either toward the appropriation, expropriation, allocation, or reallocation of governing powers.

Corporate domination will be called "hierocratic," if, and insofar as, it employs, in order to safeguard its authority, "psychic-coercion" by means of the granting or withholding of religious benefits ("hierocratic coercion"). A compulsory hierocratic association with a continuous organization will be known as a "church," if, and insofar as, its administrative staff claims a monopoly of the legitimate use of hierocratic coercion.

1. It is understood that the use of physical force is neither the only nor even the normal method of administration of political corporate groups. It means, rather, that their leaders have used all conceivable means to achieve their goals. But the threat of

force, and if need be, its actual use, is the method which is distinctive of political associations and is always the last resort when other methods have failed. But not only political corporate groups have applied and are applying physical force as a legitimate means of enforcement: it has been used just as freely by kinship groups, household groups, guilds in the Middle Ages, under certain circumstances, and everywhere by all those entitled to bear arms. The political corporate group is distinguished, in addition to its use of physical force among other means to enforce its system of authority, by the fact that the authority of its administrative staff is claimed as binding within a territorial area and that this claim is upheld by force. Whenever corporate groups which make use of force are also characterized by a claim to territorial jurisdiction—be they village communities or even only household groups, guild associations or workers associations (soviets, councils)—they must be regarded by definition to that extent as political groups.

2. It is not possible to define a political group—not even the state—in terms of the goals to which its corporate behavior is devoted. From the concern for bodily welfare to the patronage of art, there is no conceivable goal which *some* political corporation has not at some time pursued, nor is there a goal, from the protection of personal security to the administration of justice, which *all* have recognized. Consequently, the political character of a corporate group can be defined only in terms of the means not necessarily unique to it, which occasionally even becomes an end in itself, but which in the above defined specific sense is indispensable to its character, and that is the use of force. This usage does not exactly conform to everyday speech. But the latter, unless it is precisely defined, is quite useless anyway. Thus we speak of the foreign exchange policy of the *Reichsbank*,

of the financial policy of the directors of an association, of the educational policies of a community, and understand by it the systematic conduct and control of a particular problem. We are able to distinguish with much greater precision the *political* aspects of a question. Thus there is the "political" official, the "political" newspaper, the "political" party, the "political" club, the "political" revolution, and the "political" consequences of behavior, as distinguished from others, such as the economic, cultural, or religious aspects of the persons, affairs or processes in question. Used in this context, "political" means things that have to do with relations of authority within what is—according to our current usage—a political organization, the state. It refers to such things as are likely to uphold, change or overthrow, promote or inhibit, the interests of the state as distinguished from persons, things, and events which have nothing at all to do with it. This usage therefore seeks to bring out the common features of the various *means* of exercising domination customarily used within the state in enforcing its orders, exclusive of the goals they serve.

Hence it is legitimate to claim that the definition used here is only a more precise formulation of everyday usage in that it gives pointed emphasis to what is most characteristic of these means, the actual or threatened use of force. Naturally, everyday usage regards as "political" not only the groups which are the direct agents of the legitimate use of force itself but also others—for example, *wholly* peaceful groups, such as parties or clubs which attempt to influence political corporate behavior. For our purposes it seems advisable to distinguish this type of social behavior, "politically oriented" social behavior, from purely "political" behavior, i.e., the actual *corporate* behavior of political groups (as defined in Paragraph 12, Sec. 3).

3. It is appropriate to define the concept of the state in terms that conform to its modern status, since only in recent times has the state achieved full maturity. At the same time, it must be done with reference to present day values which are especially subject to change. The modern state possesses the following primary formal characteristics: an administrative and judicial authority subject to statutory change, and to which the organized corporate activity of the administrative staff, also subject to statutory change, is oriented. This system of authority claims validity not only for the members of the state, most of whom have obtained membership by birth, but also to a large extent for all conduct occurring within the area of its jurisdiction; it is thus a compulsory association with a territorial basis. In addition, the use of force today is regarded as legitimate only insofar as it is either permitted by the state or prescribed by it. Thus, it leaves to the father the right to punish his children, which is a survival of the once independent authority of the head of the household to use force even to the extent of exercising the power of life and death over children and slaves. This claim of the modern state to monopolize the use of force is a distinguishing mark as essential to it as its aspect of compulsory jurisdiction and of continuous organization.

4. The manner in which salvation is to be achieved—whether in this world or in the next, materially or spiritually—is not a decisive criterion for the formulation of the concept of a hierocratic group; rather, it is important that control over its achievement may form the basis for *spiritual domination* of human beings. On the other hand, the concept "church" is characterized even in ordinary usage by the attributes of rational compulsory association with continuous organization, and its claim of a monopolistic authority. The prevailing hierocratic territorial

and parochial organization is in accordance with the normal *striving* of a church after complete domination; the means by which such claims to monopolization are upheld vary from case to case. But unlike the political corporate group, the church historically has not felt nearly as much the need for exclusive *territorial* domination and this is especially true today. The "compulsory associational" character of the church, especially the fact of being "born" into it, is responsible for its strict differentiation from a mere "sect," whose chief distinguishing mark lies indeed in its "voluntary associational" character, admitting only those to its ranks who have the requisite religious qualities. But the details of this topic belong to the sociology of religion.